MUFFINS, NUT BREADS AND MORE
Revised Edition

Barbara Kyte and Katherine Greenberg

BRISTOL PUBLISHING ENTERPRISES
San Leandro, California

a nitty gritty® cookbook

Printed in the United States of America.

ISBN 1-55867-147-1

Cover design: Frank J. Paredes
Cover photography: John A. Benson
Food stylist: Merilee Hague Bordin
Illustrator: Richard C. Cabrera

CONTENTS

PREPARE YOUR PANTRY WITH WHOLESOME INGREDIENTS

Flour, the major ingredient in quick breads, contains gluten, which gives the bread its structure. Wheat flours, such as whole wheat and all-purpose flour, may be used separately or together to vary the texture of the bread. Whole wheat flour contains all of the wheat, including the bran and germ. It may be coarse or fine and should be stored in the refrigerator to protect the germ from turning rancid. Nonwheat flours, such as corn, oat, rye and soy, add variety to the taste and texture of quick breads and can be combined with wheat flours.

Liquids, such as milk, fruit juice and water, moisten the dry ingredients and hold the bread together.

Leavening agents, such as baking powder, baking soda, eggs and steam, make the bread rise.

Fats, such as butter, margarine and oils, add flavor and tenderness to the bread.

Sweeteners, such as honey, sugar, molasses and maple syrup, add flavor and moisture to the bread. They also aid in browning. Breads made with liquid sweeteners are more moist and stay fresh longer.

Eggs give bread rich flavor, texture and protein.

Flavorings determine the character of the bread. By varying the flavorings, you can create many variations from the same basic recipe. Flavorings include salt, extracts, herbs, spices, nuts, seeds, fruits and vegetables.

ALL ABOUT QUICK BREADS

Can you fit quick breads into your busy life? Yes! So-called "quick" because they are made without yeast, they are fast, nutritious and easy to prepare. Although quick breads are often thought of as breakfast foods because they include muffins, biscuits, pancakes, waffles and coffeecakes, they are versatile enough to eat at any time of the day. Begin with a basket of hot, tender biscuits served with butter or margarine and your favorite jam. For dinner, tempt your family with a generous square of cornbread topped with hot and hearty chili. At snack time, satisfy your craving for a sweet treat by nibbling on honey nut bread. In this book you'll find these recipes and many more.

A special chapter offers recipes for syrups, flavored butters and spreads, sauces and toppings to make your baked goods into special, out-of-the-ordinary fare.

In our collection, emphasis is on nutritious ingredients baked into treats that the whole family will enjoy. Basic recipes offer many variations, and time-saving *Quick Mix* recipes feature your own homemade baking mix (more nutritious and economical than commercially made biscuit mixes). Look for tips on preparation, measurements, ingredients, equivalents and substitutions throughout the book.

So why wait? Prepare your baking pans, preheat your oven and begin!

FOR GOOD MEASURE AND PERFECT RESULTS

Measuring ingredients accurately is an important step in making perfect quick breads. When measuring dry ingredients, you do not need to sift. Sifting removes the bran and wheat germ particles from the whole wheat flour. Just spoon the flour, baking soda and baking powder into the measuring cup or spoon and level it off with the flat edge of a knife. When measuring liquids, pour them into a glass measuring cup and examine it at eye level to check for accuracy.

The following list of equivalents will help you with your shopping and measuring.

apples	1 lb.	equals 3 medium, or 3 cups sliced or grated
apricots, dried	1 lb.	equals 3 cups dried, or 5 cups cooked
bananas	1 lb.	equals 3 whole, or 2½ cups sliced, or 1½ cups mashed
cheese	1 lb.	equals 4 cups grated
coconut	1 lb.	equals 4 cups shredded
dates, unpitted	1 lb.	equals 2½ cups unpitted, or 1¾ cups pitted
prunes	1 lb.	equals 4½ cups pitted and cooked
raisins	1 lb.	equals 3 cups
lemon	1 medium	equals 1 tbs. grated rind and 3 tbs. juice
orange	1 medium	equals 2 tbs. grated rind and ⅓ cup juice

NATURAL ADDITIONS AND SUBSTITUTIONS FOR BETTER NUTRITION

Quick breads made with natural ingredients are tastier and more nutritious. For more fiber and flavor, we prefer to use equal parts whole wheat flour and all-purpose flour in our recipes, instead of using only all-purpose flour. This ratio produces the most satisfactory results. The more whole wheat flour you use, the heavier the texture will be.

Boost the nutrition of every cup of flour by measuring 1 tbs. each instant nonfat dry milk, wheat germ and soy flour into a 1-cup measure. Fill the cup with flour and level off with the edge of a knife.

Egg substitute can be used instead of eggs to reduce fat and cholesterol. For each egg, use 1/4 cup egg substitute.

SWITCHING YOUR SWEETENERS

We also prefer honey to sugar. If you do, too, be sure to compensate for this by decreasing the quantity of liquid in the recipe. One cup of sugar equals 3/4 cup of honey. To substitute honey for sugar, decrease the liquid in the recipe by 1/4 cup. If no liquid is specified, add 1/4 cup flour.

One cup of molasses equals 1 cup of sugar. To substitute molasses for sugar, decrease the liquid in the recipe by 1/3 cup. Again, if no liquid is specified, add 1/4 cup flour.

QUICK TIPS FOR BETTER QUICK BREADS

- Avoid the last-minute rush at mealtime by mixing the dry ingredients several hours ahead, or the night before. It only takes a few minutes to add the liquid ingredients, bake and serve. If you are on a really tight schedule, you might find it convenient to keep a batch of *Quick Mix* on hand (see page 7).

- Unless otherwise specified, all the ingredients in the recipe should be at room temperature. This will insure light and tender baked goods.

- Honey will slide right out of the measuring cup if you measure the oil first. If no oil is called for in the recipe, coat the measuring cup lightly with oil before measuring the honey.

- Because you may not always have fresh buttermilk on hand, it is convenient to store a can of powdered buttermilk in your refrigerator.

- Most quick breads are best when they are served right out of the oven. When they are finished baking, serve just enough to go around and return the rest to the oven to keep warm.

- If you are not going to eat your quick breads within a few days, wrap them tightly and freeze them. They can be frozen up to 3 months. When you are ready to serve your quick breads, thaw them and warm them in a 350°F. oven.

- It takes about 5 minutes to heat muffins and biscuits, and about 10 minutes to heat loaves and coffeecakes.
- Day-old muffins and biscuits are delicious when split, toasted and spread with butter.
- For quick and easy cleanup, use any of the following: nonstick baking pans, paper liners for muffins, parchment paper or disposable foil loaf pans.

QUICK MIX

*Keep our **Quick Mix** on hand for muffins, breads, biscuits, coffeecakes, pancakes and waffles. Store, tightly covered, for up to 2 months in the refrigerator and up to 4 months in the freezer. **Quick Mix** recipes appear throughout this book.*

	Large (about 8 cups)	**Small** (about 4 cups)
whole wheat flour	3 cups	1½ cups
all-purpose flour	3 cups	1½ cups
baking powder	3 tbs.	1½ tbs.
salt	1½ tsp.	¾ tsp.
butter or margarine	1 cup	½ cup

Blend flour, baking powder and salt in a large bowl. With an electric mixer, food processor or pastry blender, cut butter into flour mixture until it resembles coarse cornmeal. Store tightly covered in the refrigerator or freezer.

BUTTERMILK QUICK MIX

*For extra flavor and nutrition, add powdered buttermilk and baking soda to the dry ingredients in the basic **Quick Mix** recipe.*

powdered buttermilk	¾ cup	⅓ cup
baking soda	1½ tsp.	¾ tsp.

MARVELOUS MUFFINS

MAKING THE PERFECT MUFFIN

The perfect muffin is moist, light and tender, with an even texture. The top of the muffin is nicely rounded and golden brown. How can you make these perfect muffins? We include a list of tips and tricks we have accumulated over the years. They work for us, and we are sure that if you follow them, they will work for you.

- Most important of all: in the last step of the recipe, when you are instructed to combine the liquid and dry ingredients, do not overmix! Overmixed muffins are tough with an uneven texture. Stir the two together only until the dry ingredients become moistened.

- Because the final step is not a mixing process, but rather a combining process, it is important to have combined the dry ingredients, and beaten together the liquid ingredients, *before* the two are combined.

- When the dry ingredients have been well combined, form a "well" in the center of them, into which you pour the liquid ingredients.

- After combining the liquid and dry ingredients, let the batter "rest" for a minute or two. This will give the leavening agents a chance to activate.

- Spoon the batter into greased or paper-lined muffin cups, filling them ⅔ full. For a special shape, try mini muffin cups, Bundt muffin cups, or for more of the crisp surface that some people consider the best part of the muffin, pans that bake muffin tops only. Remember, you must adjust the baking time according to the size and shape of the cups you use.
- Bake the muffins in a preheated oven. Test for doneness by gently pressing the center of a muffin. If it springs back, leaving little or no fingerprint, it is done. Or, you may insert a toothpick into a muffin and, if it comes out clean, the muffins are done.

QUICK MIX SAVORY MUFFINS

Makes 10

These muffins are so quick and easy to make, you can serve them often. Be sure to try some of our scrumptious variations on page 14. A small amount of sugar is added to this basic recipe to balance the flavors when using one of the variations.

½ cup milk
1 egg
2 cups *All-Purpose* or *Buttermilk Quick Mix,*
    page 7
¼ cup sugar

Preheat oven to 400°. Mix milk and egg together well. Add to *Quick Mix* and sugar. Stir until just moistened. Fill greased or paper-lined muffin cups ⅔ full. Bake for 20 minutes, or until brown.

BASIC SAVORY MUFFINS

Start with the ingredients for a perfect muffin and be creative with our variations on page 14. A small amount of honey (or sugar) balances the flavors when using one of the variations.

¾ cup whole wheat or all-purpose flour
1 cup all-purpose flour
2½ tsp. baking powder
½ tsp. salt
½ cup milk when using honey (¾ cup milk when using sugar)
1 egg
⅓ cup vegetable oil
¼ cup honey or sugar

Preheat oven to 400°. Stir together flours, baking powder and salt. Mix milk, egg, oil and honey together well. Add liquid mixture to dry ingredients. Stir until just moistened. Fill greased or paper-lined muffin cups ⅔ full. Bake for 20 minutes, or until golden brown.

SAVORY MUFFIN VARIATIONS

*For variety, add one of the following to the dry ingredients in our **Quick Mix Savory Muffins** or **Basic Savory Muffins** recipes on pages 12 and 13.*

- 3 tbs. thinly sliced green onion
- $1/4$ tsp. dried dill, $1/2$ tsp. dried oregano and 1 tbs. snipped fresh parsley
- $1/2$ cup shredded cheddar cheese
- $1/2$ cup shredded Swiss cheese and 1 tsp. caraway seeds
- $1/3$ cup crumbled blue cheese, 2 tbs. minced red onion and $1/4$ cup chopped walnuts
- $1/2$ cup grated carrot, $1/4$ cup sunflower kernels, $1/4$ tsp. dried thyme or $1/2$ tsp. dried tarragon
- $1/2$ cup sunflower kernels
- (if you aren't using *Buttermilk Quick Mix*) $1/4$ cup powdered buttermilk and $1/2$ tsp. baking soda; or replace milk with buttermilk and add $1/2$ tsp. baking soda

Also, if desired

- Before baking, sprinkle the top of each muffin with about $1/4$ tsp. paprika, Parmesan cheese or sesame seeds.

OATMEAL MUFFINS

Serve these muffins hot with sweet butter and jam — so good! And full of healthy fiber, too.

1 cup whole wheat or all-purpose flour
1 cup quick-cooking oats
2½ tsp. baking powder
½ tsp. baking soda
½ tsp. salt
¼ cup brown sugar, firmly packed
1 egg
¾ cup buttermilk
⅓ cup vegetable oil

Preheat oven to 400°. Stir together flour, oats, baking powder, baking soda, salt and brown sugar. Mix egg, buttermilk and oil together well. Add liquid mixture to dry ingredients. Stir until just moistened. Fill greased or paper-lined muffin cups ⅔ full. Bake for 20 minutes, or until golden brown.

GRANOLA MUFFINS

Use your favorite granola cereal for a lunch box treat.

2 cups *All-Purpose* or *Buttermilk Quick Mix,* page 7
1 cup granola
1 egg
1 cup milk
2 tsp. cinnamon or nutmeg, optional

Preheat oven to 400°. Stir together *Quick Mix* and granola. Mix egg and milk together well. Add liquid mixture to dry ingredients, except cinnamon or nutmeg. Stir until just moistened. Fill greased or paper-lined muffin cups 2/3 full. If desired, sprinkle batter lightly with cinnamon or nutmeg. Bake for 20 minutes, or until golden brown.

STREUSEL MUFFINS

This delightful breakfast muffin is like a mini coffee cake.

1¾ cups all-purpose flour
2½ tsp. baking powder
½ tsp. baking soda
½ tsp. salt
1 tsp. nutmeg

½ cup sugar
¾ cup buttermilk
1 egg
⅓ cup vegetable oil
Streusel Topping, follows

Preheat oven to 400°. Stir together flour, baking powder, baking soda, salt, nutmeg and sugar. Mix buttermilk, egg and oil together well. Add liquid mixture to dry ingredients. Stir until just moistened. Rest batter for 1 minute. Fill greased or paper-lined muffin cups ⅔ full. Sprinkle *Streusel Topping* on muffin batter. Bake for 20 minutes, or until golden brown.

STREUSEL TOPPING

3 tbs. all-purpose flour
¼ cup brown sugar, firmly packed
½ tsp. cinnamon

¼ tsp. nutmeg
¼ cup chopped pecans or walnuts
2 tbs. butter or margarine

Combine dry ingredients. Add butter and cut in until mixture is crumbly.

OLD-FASHIONED BRAN MUFFINS

Makes 12

These delicious muffins taste just like the ones Grandma used to make! You can find unprocessed bran in health food stores, and in some large supermarkets.

1 cup whole wheat or all-purpose flour
1 cup unprocessed bran
2½ tsp. baking powder
½ tsp. baking soda
½ tsp. salt
½ cup raisins or chopped dates
¼ cup sugar or honey
1 egg
⅔ cup buttermilk
¼ cup vegetable oil
¼ cup molasses

Preheat oven to 400°. Stir together flour, bran, baking powder, baking soda, salt, raisins and sugar. Mix egg, buttermilk, oil and molasses together well. Add liquid mixture to dry ingredients. Stir until just moistened. Fill greased or paper-lined muffin cups ⅔ full. Bake for 20 minutes, or until done.

MAKE-AHEAD BRAN MUFFINS

The batter for these wholesome muffins will keep for 2 weeks in the refrigerator.

¾ cup boiling water when using honey
   (1 cup boiling water when using sugar)
2 cups all-bran cereal
1 cup crushed shredded wheat cereal
1¼ cups whole wheat flour
1¼ cups all-purpose flour
2½ tsp. baking soda

1 tsp. salt
1 cup raisins or any chopped dried fruit
2 eggs
½ cup vegetable oil
⅓ cup molasses
¾ cup honey, or 1 cup sugar
1 cup buttermilk

Preheat oven to 400°. Pour boiling water over cereals and set aside. Combine flours, baking soda and salt. Mix together raisins, eggs, oil, molasses and honey. Add to dry ingredients. Stir just until moistened. Alternately add cereal mixture and buttermilk. When ready to bake, fill greased or paper-lined muffin cups ⅔ full. Bake for 20 minutes, or until done.

CORN MUFFINS

Serve these muffins piping hot, spread with butter and drizzled with honey.

½ cup whole wheat or all-purpose flour
½ cup all-purpose flour
1 cup yellow cornmeal
1 tbs. baking powder
¾ tsp. salt
¼ cup sugar or honey
1 cup milk
1 egg
¼ cup vegetable oil

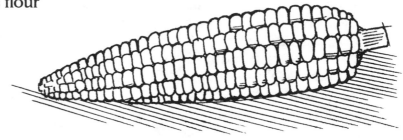

Preheat oven to 400°. Stir together flours, cornmeal, baking powder, salt and sugar. Mix milk, egg and oil together well. Add liquid mixture to dry ingredients. Stir until just moistened. Rest batter for 5 minutes. Fill greased or paper-lined muffin cups ⅔ full. Bake for 15 to 20 minutes, or until done.

CORN MUFFIN VARIATIONS

*Vary **Corn Muffins** on page 20 to make many different muffins.*

Add one of these items to the dry ingredients.

- 1/4 cup crumbled crisp bacon
- 1/4 cup thinly sliced green onions
- 3/4 tsp. dried dill weed
- 1/2 cup grated cheese
- 3 tbs. chopped green chiles
- 1/4 cup finely chopped ham

Try these ideas.

- Fill muffin cups 1/2 full with batter. Drop 1/2 teaspoon jam in each cup and add batter to fill each cup 2/3 full, covering jam with batter.
- Before baking, sprinkle the top of each muffin with sesame seeds or a dash of paprika.

BLUEBERRY CORN MUFFINS

Cornmeal adds a wonderful texture to these scrumptious muffins.

1½ cups all-purpose flour
¼ cup cornmeal
2½ tsp. baking powder
½ tsp. baking soda
½ tsp. salt
⅓ cup sugar
¾ cup buttermilk
1 egg
⅓ cup vegetable oil
1 cup blueberries

Preheat oven to 400°. Stir together flour, cornmeal, baking powder, baking soda, salt and sugar. Mix buttermilk, egg and oil together well. Add liquid mixture to dry ingredients. Stir until just moistened. Gently fold in blueberries. Fill greased or paper-lined muffin cups ⅔ full. Bake for 20 minutes, or until golden brown.

TOMATO CORN MUFFINS

The flavor of these savory muffins is accented with basil.

1¼ cups all-purpose flour
¾ cup cornmeal
2½ tsp. baking powder
½ tsp. salt
¼ cup sugar
1 tsp. dried basil
¾ cup milk
1 egg
⅓ cup vegetable oil
½ cup chopped tomato
grated Parmesan cheese

Preheat oven to 400°. Stir together flour, cornmeal, baking powder, salt, sugar and basil. Mix milk, egg and oil together well. Add liquid mixture and chopped tomato to dry ingredients and stir until just moistened. Fill greased or paper-lined muffin cups ⅔ full. Sprinkle top of each muffin with Parmesan cheese. Bake for 20 minutes, or until golden brown.

PESTO MUFFINS

Pesto is becoming more and more popular, and for good reason. Here it is in a muffin. Make pesto with the recipe on page 146, or buy it ready-made in the refrigerator case of your supermarket, usually near the fresh pasta.

¾ cup whole wheat or all-purpose flour
1 cup all-purpose flour
2½ tsp. baking powder
½ tsp. salt
2 tbs. sugar
¼ cup pine nuts

¾ cup milk
1 egg
⅓ cup vegetable oil
2 tbs. pesto
grated Parmesan cheese

Preheat oven to 400°. Stir together flours, baking powder, salt, sugar and pine nuts. Mix milk, egg, oil and pesto together well. Add liquid mixture to dry ingredients and stir until just moistened. Fill greased or paper-lined muffin cups ⅔ full. Sprinkle top of batter with Parmesan cheese. Bake for 20 minutes or until golden brown.

ZUCCHINI CHEESE MUFFINS

These flavorful muffins will enhance a bowl of hearty soup, a crispy salad or any simple meal. Or bake them in mini muffin cups and serve them as hors d'oeuvres.

2 cups all-purpose flour
1 tbs. baking powder
½ tsp. salt
2 tbs. sugar
2 tbs. minced green onion
½ cup grated sharp cheddar cheese
¾ cup shredded zucchini
1 egg
¾ cup milk
¼ cup vegetable oil

Preheat oven to 400°. Stir together flour, baking powder, salt, sugar, green onion, cheese and zucchini. Mix egg, milk and oil together well. Add liquid mixture to dry ingredients. Stir until just moistened. Fill greased or paper-lined muffin cups ⅔ full. Bake for 20 minutes, or until golden brown.

QUICK MIX SWEET MUFFINS

Makes 10

This version using Quick Mix provides a basic, sweet muffin. See page 28 for several delicious variations.

½ cup sugar or honey
½ cup milk when using honey (⅔ cup milk when using sugar)
1 egg
2 cups *All-Purpose* or *Buttermilk Quick Mix,* page 7

Preheat oven to 400°. Mix sugar or honey, milk and egg together well. Add liquid mixture to *Quick Mix*. Stir until just moistened. Fill greased or paper-lined muffin cups ⅔ full. Bake for 20 minutes, or until golden brown.

BASIC SWEET MUFFINS

Produce tender muffins with this basic recipe; the variations on page 28 offer many creative possibilities.

¾ cup whole wheat or all-purpose flour
1 cup all-purpose flour
2½ tsp. baking powder
½ tsp. salt
½ cup milk when using honey (¾ cup milk when using sugar)
1 egg
⅓ cup vegetable oil
½ cup honey or sugar

Preheat oven to 400°. Stir together flours, baking powder and salt. Mix milk, egg, oil and honey or sugar together well. Add this mixture to dry ingredients. Stir until just moistened. Rest batter for 1 minute. Fill greased or paper-lined muffin cups ⅔ full. Bake for 20 minutes, or until golden brown.

SWEET MUFFIN VARIATIONS
Use these additions to vary the basic recipes on pages 28 and 29.

Add one of the following to the dry ingredients.
- ½ cup chopped walnuts or other nuts
- ½ cup raisins, dates, dried cherries, dried cranberries or any chopped dried fruit
- ½ cup grated peeled apple
- 1 cup blueberries
- 1 tbs. grated orange or lemon rind (zest)
- 1 tsp. cinnamon or nutmeg

Try these ideas.

Jam Muffins. Place 1 tsp. jam on top of each muffin before baking. Or, fill muffin cups ½ full with batter, drop 1 tsp. jam on each and cover with batter to fill cup ⅔ full.

Banana Muffins. Fill each muffin cup ½ full with batter. Place a slice of banana on batter and cover with more batter to fill cup ⅔ full.

Sugar-Topped Muffins. Sprinkle top of muffin batter with sugar before baking.

APPLE RAISIN MUFFINS

Makes 12

For all you apple lovers, this muffin has a tempting, spicy apple flavor.

2 cups *All-Purpose* or *Buttermilk Quick Mix*, page 7
½ tsp. cinnamon
½ cup raisins
½ cup brown sugar, firmly packed
½ cup grated peeled apple
1 egg
½ cup milk

Preheat oven to 400°. Combine *Quick Mix*, cinnamon, raisins, brown sugar and grated apple. Mix egg and milk together well. Add liquid mixture to dry ingredients. Stir until just moistened. Fill greased or paper-lined muffin cups ⅔ full. Bake for 20 minutes, or until golden brown.

BLUEBERRY GINGER MUFFINS

You'll love this delicious and unusual combination.

2½ cups all-purpose flour
1 tbs. baking powder
½ tsp. baking soda
½ tsp. salt
⅓ cup sugar
1 tsp. cinnamon

½ tsp. ground ginger
1 egg
1 cup buttermilk
¼ cup vegetable oil
½ cup dark molasses
1 cup blueberries

Preheat oven to 400°. Stir together flour, baking powder, baking soda, salt, sugar, cinnamon and ginger. Mix egg, buttermilk, oil and molasses together well. Add liquid mixture to dry ingredients. Stir until just moistened. Gently fold in blueberries. Fill greased or paper-lined muffin cups ⅔ full. Bake for 20 minutes, or until done.

BANANA OATMEAL MUFFINS

Makes about 16

Wake up your family with the mouth-watering aroma of these healthful breakfast muffins. Children are particularly fond of them.

1½ cups all-purpose flour
1 cup quick-cooking oats
2 tsp. baking powder
1 tsp. baking soda
½ tsp. salt
1 egg
½ cup milk when using honey (¾ cup milk when using sugar)
⅓ cup vegetable oil
½ cup honey or sugar
⅔ cup mashed banana

Preheat oven to 400°. Stir together flour, oats, baking powder, baking soda and salt. Mix egg, milk, oil, honey or sugar and mashed banana together well. Add liquid mixture to dry ingredients. Stir until just moistened. Fill greased or paper-lined muffin cups ⅔ full. Bake for 20 minutes, or until golden brown.

COCONUT PINEAPPLE MUFFINS

These muffins are as light as a tropical breeze.

2 cups all-purpose flour
1 tbs. baking powder
½ tsp. salt
½ cup sugar
½ cup flaked coconut
1 egg
¼ cup vegetable oil
⅓ cup milk
1 tsp. vanilla extract
1 can (8 oz.) crushed pineapple with juice

Preheat oven to 400°. Stir together flour, baking powder, salt, sugar and coconut. Mix egg, oil, milk, vanilla and pineapple together well. Add liquid mixture to dry ingredients. Stir until just moistened. Fill greased or paper-lined muffin cups ⅔ full. Bake for 20 minutes, or until golden brown.

ORANGE DATE MUFFINS

What a treat with afternoon tea!

1 cup whole wheat or all-purpose flour
1 cup all-purpose flour
2½ tsp. baking powder
½ tsp. salt
1 tbs. grated orange rind (zest)
⅔ cup chopped dates
1 egg
¾ cup orange juice
⅓ cup vegetable oil
¼ cup honey or sugar

Preheat oven to 400°. Stir together flours, baking powder, salt, orange zest and dates. Mix egg, orange juice, oil and honey or sugar together well. Add liquid mixture to dry ingredients. Stir until just moistened. Fill greased or paper-lined muffin cups ⅔ full. Bake for 20 minutes, or until golden brown.

CRANBERRY ORANGE MUFFINS

These tangy muffins are the perfect complement to a holiday dinner.

2 cups *All-Purpose* or *Buttermilk Quick Mix,* page 7
½ cup sugar
1 tbs. grated orange rind (zest)
½ cup chopped pecans or walnuts
1 egg
¼ cup orange juice
1 can (8 oz.) whole cranberry sauce

Preheat oven to 400°. Stir together *Quick Mix,* sugar, grated orange zest and chopped nuts. Mix egg, orange juice and cranberry sauce together well. Add liquid mixture to dry ingredients. Stir until just moistened. Fill greased or paper-lined muffin cups ⅔ full. Bake for 25 minutes, or until golden brown.

MOLASSES PRUNE MUFFINS

Molasses enhances the flavor of the prunes in this nutritious muffin.

2 cups *All-Purpose* or *Buttermilk Quick Mix,* page 7
½ cup chopped nuts
½ cup chopped dried prunes
1 egg
½ cup milk
½ cup dark molasses

Preheat oven to 400°. Combine *Quick Mix*, nuts and dried prunes. Mix egg, milk and molasses together well. Add liquid mixture to dry ingredients. Stir until just moistened. Fill greased or paper-lined muffin cups ⅔ full. Bake for 20 minutes, or until golden brown.

PERSIMMON MUFFINS

There are two kinds of persimmons. The Hachiya, or Japanese persimmon, is large and round, with a pointed base, and is very astringent. The Fuyu persimmon is smaller with a tomato shape, and is creamy and tangy-sweet. Use the Fuyu persimmons for this recipe. When they are in season, you can freeze them whole or pureed to have on hand for baking these delicious muffins.

1 cup whole wheat or all-purpose flour
1 cup all-purpose flour
1 tbs. baking powder
½ tsp. salt
½ tsp. cinnamon
½ tsp. nutmeg
¼ tsp. ground cloves

½ cup raisins or chopped dates
1 egg
½ cup milk
⅓ cup vegetable oil
½ cup honey
½ cup mashed persimmon pulp

Preheat oven to 400°. Stir together flours, baking powder, salt, cinnamon, nutmeg, cloves and raisins. Mix egg, milk, vegetable oil, honey and persimmon pulp together well. Add to dry ingredients. Stir until just moistened. Fill greased or paper-lined muffin cups ⅔ full. Bake for 20 minutes, or until golden brown.

MAPLE NUT MUFFINS

Makes 12

For a change, make miniature muffins. Children love them. This recipe makes 42 miniature muffins.

1 cup whole wheat or all-purpose flour
1 cup all-purpose flour
2½ tsp. baking powder
¼ tsp. baking soda
½ tsp. salt
½ cup sugar

½ cup chopped nuts
1 egg
½ cup milk
¼ cup maple syrup
¼ cup vegetable oil
½ cup sour cream

Preheat oven to 400°. Stir together flours, baking powder, baking soda, salt, sugar and nuts. Mix egg, milk, syrup, oil and sour cream together well. Add liquid mixture to dry ingredients. Stir until just moistened. Fill greased or paper-lined muffin cups ⅔ full. Bake for 20 minutes, or 15 minutes for miniature muffins.

LEMON YOGURT MUFFINS

Lemon yogurt is our choice for this moist muffin. Be inventive and try your favorite yogurt flavor.

2 cups all-purpose flour
2½ tsp. baking powder
½ tsp. baking soda
½ tsp. salt
1 tbs. grated lemon rind (zest)
1 egg
¼ cup vegetable oil
⅓ cup honey
1 carton (8 oz.) lemon yogurt

Preheat oven to 400°. Stir together flour, baking powder, baking soda, salt and grated lemon zest. Mix egg, oil, honey and yogurt together well. Add liquid mixture to dry ingredients. Stir until just moistened. Fill greased or paper-lined muffin cups ⅔ full. Bake for 18 minutes, or until golden brown.

LOAVES SAVORY AND SWEET

MAKING THE PERFECT LOAF

These tips should make baking quick bread loaves fun and easy.

- Like muffins, loaf batter should not be overmixed. When you combine liquid and dry ingredients, try to use as few strokes as possible.
- If the recipe calls for butter or margarine, allow it to soften at room temperature for a few hours before you use it. Then beat it until it becomes creamy.
- If you always grease and flour your pans, loaves can be removed easily. Or line your pans with parchment paper or buttered brown paper.
- Check your bread halfway through the baking time. If the top is browning too rapidly, cover it with aluminum foil for the remaining baking time.
- The loaf is done when a toothpick inserted into the thickest part comes out clean.
- Cool the bread in the pan for about 10 minutes. Remove from the pan and cool completely on a wire rack.
- Your bread will stay fresh longer if you wrap it securely in aluminum foil.

WHOLE WHEAT BREAD

Make delicious sandwiches with this hearty whole wheat bread.

2 cups whole wheat flour
2 tsp. baking powder
1 tsp. baking soda
½ tsp. salt
½ cup raisins, optional
1 cup buttermilk
1 egg
¼ cup vegetable oil
2 tbs. honey or sugar

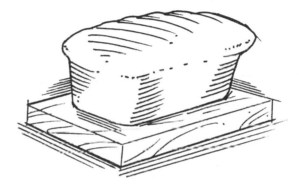

Preheat oven to 350°. Combine flour, baking powder, baking soda, salt and raisins. Mix buttermilk, egg, oil and honey together well. Add liquid mixture to dry ingredients. Stir just until blended. Pour batter into a greased, floured loaf pan (9-x-5-x-3 inches). Bake for 45 minutes or until bread tests done. Cool in pan for 10 minutes. Turn out on a wire rack to cool completely.

SUPER BREAD

This nutritious bread contains many healthy ingredients.

¾ cup soy flour
1 cup whole wheat or all-purpose flour
1 cup all-purpose flour
½ cup wheat germ
¼ cup unprocessed bran
⅓ cup instant nonfat dry milk
1 tbs. baking powder
1 tbs. baking soda
½ tsp. salt

½ cup chopped dates or raisins
½ cup chopped nuts
1 cup yogurt
1 egg, well beaten
¼ cup vegetable oil
¼ cup molasses
¼ cup honey
½ cup orange juice

Preheat oven to 350°. Stir together flours, wheat germ, bran, dry milk, baking powder, baking soda, salt, dates and nuts. Mix yogurt, egg, oil, molasses, honey and orange juice together well. Add liquid mixture to dry ingredients. Stir until just blended. Spread batter into a greased, floured loaf pan (9-x-5-x-3 inches). Bake for 1 hour, or until bread tests done. Cover loosely with foil during the last 15 minutes of baking to prevent excess browning. Cool in pan for about 10 minutes. Turn out on a wire rack to cool completely.

RAISIN OATMEAL BREAD

Toast a slice of this delectable bread and serve it with one of our tempting spreads on page 144.

2 cups all-purpose flour
1 cup quick-cooking oats
1 tbs. baking powder
½ tsp. baking soda
½ tsp. salt
1 cup raisins
1¼ cups buttermilk
1 egg, well beaten
¼ cup molasses or honey
¼ cup vegetable oil

Preheat oven to 350°. Stir together flour, oats, baking powder, baking soda, salt and raisins. Mix buttermilk, egg, molasses and oil together well. Add liquid mixture to dry ingredients. Stir until just blended. Pour batter into a greased, floured loaf pan (9-x-5-x-3 inches). Bake for 60 minutes, or until bread tests done. Cool in pan for about 10 minutes. Turn out on a wire rack to cool completely.

ZUCCHINI HERB BREAD

A savory blend of herbs enhances this satisfying bread. If you have fresh herbs, triple the amount called for.

1½ cups whole wheat or all-purpose flour

1½ cups all-purpose flour

1 tbs. baking powder

½ tsp. salt

1 tsp. dried oregano

1 tsp. dried basil

¼ tsp. garlic powder, optional

1 tbs. minced onion

½ cup grated Parmesan cheese

1 cup grated zucchini

1¼ cups milk

1 egg

¼ cup vegetable oil

Preheat oven to 350°. Stir together flours, baking powder, salt, oregano, basil, garlic powder, minced onion and Parmesan cheese. Combine zucchini, milk, egg and vegetable oil. Add liquid mixture to dry ingredients. Stir just until blended. Pour batter into a greased, floured loaf pan (9-x-5-x-3 inches). Bake for 1 hour and 15 minutes or until done. Cool in pan for about 10 minutes. Turn out on a wire rack to cool completely.

RYE CHEESE BREAD

This quick bread is just right for a deli sandwich.

1 cup rye flour
1 cup all-purpose flour
1 tbs. baking powder
½ tsp. salt
1 tsp. dried dill weed
1 tbs. caraway seeds
1 cup shredded Swiss cheese
1 cup milk
1 egg
¼ cup vegetable oil
2 tbs. honey or sugar

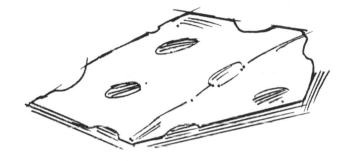

Preheat oven to 350°. Stir together flours, baking powder, salt, dill, caraway seeds and cheese. Mix milk, egg, oil and honey together well. Add liquid mixture to dry ingredients. Stir until just blended. Pour batter into a greased, floured loaf pan (9-x-5-x-3 inches). Bake for 55 minutes, or until bread tests done. Cool in pan for about 10 minutes. Turn out on a wire rack to cool completely.

PIZZA BREAD

This bread makes a meal in itself, or you can serve it cut into small squares for a tasty appetizer.

1 cup whole wheat or all-purpose flour
1 cup all-purpose flour
1 tbs. baking powder
½ tsp. salt
1½ tsp. dried oregano
¾ cup milk

1 egg
¼ cup vegetable oil
1 tbs. honey or sugar
Pizza Sauce, follows
Topping Suggestions, follow

Preheat oven to 400°. Stir together flours, baking powder, salt and oregano. Mix milk, egg, oil and honey together well. Add liquid mixture to dry ingredients. Stir until just blended. Spread batter in a greased baking pan (9-x-9-x-2 inches). Spread *Pizza Sauce* over batter. Cover with 1 or more topping ingredients. Bake for 30 minutes, or until done.

PIZZA SAUCE
1 can (6 oz.) tomato paste
¼ tsp. dried basil

¼ tsp. dried oregano
¼ tsp. garlic powder

Combine all ingredients. Spread over batter.

TOPPING SUGGESTIONS

- ½ cup sliced mushrooms
- ½ cup sliced green peppers
- ¼ cup sliced black olives
- 5 minced anchovies
- ¼ cup sliced onions
- ½ cup diced pepperoni, prosciutto or salami
- 1 cup shredded mozzarella cheese

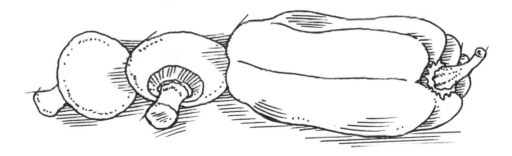

MEXICAN CORNBREAD

Here's perfect accompaniment to any south-of-the-border meal. Try it with our **Chili Topper***, page 148.*

½ cup whole wheat or all-purpose flour
½ cup all-purpose flour
¾ cup yellow cornmeal
1 tbs. baking powder
½ tsp. salt
1 tsp. chili powder
2 tbs. minced onion
¼ cup chopped green chiles, optional

1 cup drained, Mexican-style whole
   kernel corn
1 cup shredded cheddar cheese
1 cup milk
1 egg
2 tbs. vegetable oil
2 tbs. honey or sugar

Preheat oven to 400°. Stir together flours, cornmeal, baking powder, salt, chili powder, onion, chiles, corn and cheese. Mix milk, egg, oil and honey together well. Add liquid mixture to dry ingredients. Stir until just blended. Rest batter for 5 minutes. Pour batter into a greased (9-x-9-x-2 inch) baking pan. Bake for 25 minutes, or until golden brown.

QUICK BOSTON BROWN BREAD

This version of an old favorite goes together quickly.

1 cup whole wheat flour
1 cup all-purpose flour
1 tsp. baking powder
1 tsp. baking soda
½ tsp. salt
¼ cup sugar
1 cup buttermilk
1 egg
¾ cup light or dark molasses
¾ cup raisins

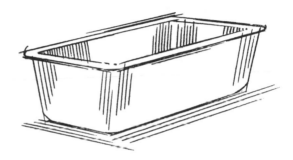

Preheat oven to 350°. Combine flours, baking powder, baking soda, salt and sugar. Mix buttermilk, egg, molasses and raisins well. Add to dry ingredients and stir until blended. Pour batter into a greased, floured loaf pan (9-x-5-x-3 inches). Bake for 55 to 60 minutes or until bread tests done. Cool in pan for 10 minutes. Turn out on a wire rack to cool completely.

CLASSIC NUT BREAD

Makes 1 loaf

Our favorite nut bread lends itself to many variations (see page 49).

1 cup whole wheat or all-purpose flour
1 cup all-purpose flour
1 tbs. baking powder
½ tsp. salt
1 cup chopped walnuts
⅔ cup honey, or ¾ cup sugar
¾ cup milk when using honey (1 cup milk when using sugar)
1 egg
¼ cup vegetable oil

Preheat oven to 350°. Stir together flours, baking powder, salt and nuts. Mix honey, milk, egg and oil together well. Add liquid mixture to dry ingredients. Stir until just blended. Pour batter into a greased, floured loaf pan (9-x-5-x-3 inches). Bake for 50 minutes, or until bread tests done. Cool in pan for about 10 minutes. Turn out on a wire rack to cool completely.

CLASSIC NUT BREAD VARIATIONS

*Try a different variation each time you bake **Classic Nut Bread**, page 50.*

- **Apricot Nut Bread.** Add ¾ cup chopped dried apricots. Or use any dried fruit, such as dried cherries, dried cranberries, chopped dried apples or pears.
- **Date Nut Bread.** Substitute ¾ cup brown sugar for ¾ cup sugar and add ½ cup chopped dates.
- **Orange Nut Bread.** Substitute orange juice for milk and add 2 tbs. grated orange rind (zest).
- **Lemon Nut Bread.** Add 1 tbs. grated lemon rind (zest).
- **Spice Nut Bread.** Add ¼ tsp. ground cloves, plus ½ tsp. cinnamon and ½ tsp. nutmeg.
- **Pecan, Almond and Walnut Bread.** Replace 1 cup chopped walnuts with ⅓ cup **each** chopped pecans, almonds and walnuts.

ORANGE BRAN BREAD

This is a perfect choice for breakfast.

2/3 cup honey
1 cup orange juice
1½ cups all-bran cereal
1 cup whole wheat or all-purpose flour
1 cup all-purpose flour
1 tbs. baking powder
½ tsp. salt

1 tsp. cinnamon
¼ tsp. ground cloves
1 tbs. grated orange rind (zest)
1 cup golden raisins
1 egg
¼ cup vegetable oil

Preheat oven to 350°. Mix honey, orange juice and bran cereal. Combine flours, baking powder, salt, cinnamon, cloves, orange zest and raisins in a large bowl. Mix egg and oil with bran mixture. Stir into dry ingredients. Pour batter into greased, floured loaf pan (9-x-5-x-3 inches). Bake for 60 minutes or until done.

BRAN APPLESAUCE LOAF

This nutritious bread makes a great mid-morning snack.

½ cup all-bran cereal
1 cup applesauce
½ cup butter or margarine, softened
¾ cup honey
1 egg
2 cups all-purpose flour

2 tsp. baking powder
1 tsp. baking soda
½ tsp. salt
1 tsp. cinnamon
¼ tsp. ground cloves
½ cup raisins

Preheat oven to 350°. Combine all-bran cereal and applesauce. Set aside. Cream butter and honey. Add egg and mix well. Stir together flour, baking powder, baking soda, salt, cinnamon and cloves. Add dry ingredients to creamed mixture alternately with applesauce-bran cereal mixture. Mix until just blended. Stir in raisins. Pour batter into a greased, floured loaf pan (9-x-5-x-3 inches). Bake for 60 minutes, or until bread tests done. Cool in pan for about 10 minutes. Turn out on a wire rack to cool completely.

HONEY WALNUT BREAD

Makes 1 loaf

Serve this bread warm from the oven, or toast it to bring out the flavors.

1/4 cup butter or margarine
1 cup honey
1 egg
1 cup milk
1 1/4 cups whole wheat or all-purpose flour
1 1/4 cups all-purpose flour
1 1/2 tsp. baking soda
1/2 tsp. salt
1 cup coarsely chopped walnuts
walnut halves, optional

Preheat oven to 350°. Cream butter, adding honey in a fine stream. Beat in egg and milk. Combine flours, baking soda and salt. Add to creamed ingredients, mixing well. Stir in chopped nuts. Pour batter into a greased, floured loaf pan (9-x-5-x-3 inches). Garnish the top with walnut halves if desired. Bake for 70 minutes or until bread tests done. Cool in the pan for about 10 minutes. Turn out on a wire rack to cool completely.

MORAGA PEAR AND WALNUT BREAD

Makes 1 loaf

Living in the midst of pear and walnut orchards in Moraga, California, inspired us to create this recipe.

1 cup whole wheat or all-purpose flour
1 cup all-purpose flour
1 tbs. baking powder
½ tsp. salt
½ tsp. cinnamon
¼ tsp. nutmeg
¼ tsp. ground cloves

1 cup chopped pears
1 cup coarsely chopped walnuts
½ cup milk
1 egg
¼ cup vegetable oil
¾ cup honey

Preheat oven to 350°. Stir together flours, baking powder, salt, cinnamon, nutmeg, cloves, pears and walnuts. Mix milk, egg, oil and honey together well. Add liquid mixture to dry ingredients. Stir until just blended. Pour batter into a greased, floured loaf pan (9-x-5-x-3 inches). Bake for 65 minutes, or until done. Cool in pan for about 10 minutes. Turn out on a wire rack to cool completely.

BANANA NUT BREAD

Just about everybody's favorite!

Makes 1 loaf

1/3 cup butter or margarine, softened
3/4 cup sugar
1 egg
1 cup mashed bananas
2 cups all-purpose flour
2 1/2 tsp. baking powder
1/4 tsp. baking soda
1/2 tsp. salt
1 cup chopped pecans or walnuts
1/2 cup buttermilk

Preheat oven to 350°. Cream butter and sugar. Mix in egg and bananas. Stir together flour, baking powder, baking soda, salt and nuts. Add dry ingredients to creamed mixture alternately with buttermilk. Stir until just blended. Pour batter into a greased, floured loaf pan (9-x-5-x-3 inches). Bake for 65 minutes, or until bread tests done. Cool in pan for about 10 minutes. Turn out on a wire rack to cool completely.

POPPY SEED LOAF

Brown sugar and buttermilk combined with the sweet crunch of poppy seeds create a light loaf with distinctive texture.

1/4 cup butter or margarine, softened
1 cup dark brown sugar, firmly packed
1 egg
2 tsp. vanilla extract
2 cups all-purpose flour
2 tsp. baking powder
1 tsp. baking soda
1/2 tsp. salt
3 tbs. poppy seeds
1 cup buttermilk

Preheat oven to 350°. Cream butter and sugar. Stir in egg and vanilla. Combine flour, baking powder, baking soda, salt and poppy seeds. Add dry ingredients to creamed mixture alternately with buttermilk. Stir until just blended. Pour batter into a greased, floured loaf pan (9-x-5-x-3 inches). Bake for 60 minutes, or until bread tests done. Cool in pan for about 10 minutes. Turn out on a wire rack to cool completely.

TUTTI-FRUTTI NUT BREAD

This festive bread with a delightful blend of fruit and nuts is perfect for holidays.

1 cup whole wheat or all-purpose flour
1 cup all-purpose flour
1 tbs. baking powder
1/2 tsp. salt
3/4 cup brown sugar, firmly packed
1/2 cup grated apple
1/2 cup chopped dried apricots

1/2 cup chopped dates
1 cup chopped nuts
3/4 cup milk
1 egg
1/4 cup vegetable oil
3 tbs. brandy, optional

Preheat oven to 350°. Stir together flours, baking powder, salt, brown sugar, grated apple, apricots, dates and nuts. Mix milk, egg and oil together well. Add to dry ingredients and stir until just blended. Pour batter in a greased, floured loaf pan (9-x-5-x-3 inches). Bake for 1 hour, or until bread tests done. If desired, pour brandy over loaf while still warm. Turn out on a wire rack to cool.

SHERRIED PUMPKIN LOAF

Makes 1 loaf

This spicy bread is wonderful in the fall for breakfast, for snacks or even for dessert. Use this loaf, or any of our sweet loaves, to make tasty little tea sandwiches spread with cream cheese.

1 cup whole wheat or all-purpose flour
1 cup all-purpose flour
1 tbs. baking powder
½ tsp. salt
½ tsp. cinnamon
½ tsp. nutmeg
¼ tsp. ground cloves

1 cup sugar
1 cup chopped pecans or walnuts
½ cup cream sherry
2 eggs
½ cup vegetable oil
1 cup canned pumpkin

Preheat oven to 350°. Combine flours, baking powder, salt, cinnamon, nutmeg, cloves, sugar and nuts. Mix sherry, eggs, oil and pumpkin well. Add to dry ingredients. Stir just until blended. Pour batter into a greased, floured loaf pan (9-x-5-x-3 inches). Bake for 65 minutes or until done. Cool in pan for about 10 minutes. Turn out on a wire rack to cool completely.

CHEDDAR BEER BREAD

Beer gives this bread a slight sourdough flavor.

2½ cups all-purpose flour
1½ tsp. baking soda
½ tsp. salt
½ tsp. nutmeg
¾ cup brown sugar, firmly packed
1 cup shredded cheddar cheese
1 cup chopped walnuts
1¼ cups beer
1 egg
¼ cup vegetable oil

Preheat oven to 350°. Stir together flour, baking soda, salt, nutmeg, brown sugar, cheese and nuts. Mix beer, egg and oil together well. Add liquid mixture to dry ingredients. Stir until just blended. Pour batter into a greased, floured loaf pan (9-x-5-x-3 inches). Bake for 60 minutes, or until bread tests done. Cool in pan for about 10 minutes. Turn out on a wire rack to cool completely.

COCONUT BREAD

Toasting the coconut enhances this bread's nut-like flavor.

1 cup shredded coconut
2 cups all-purpose flour
1 tbs. baking powder
½ tsp. salt
1 cup milk
1 egg
¼ cup vegetable oil
¾ cup sugar
1 tsp. vanilla extract

Preheat oven 350°. Place coconut in a large, shallow baking pan in oven. Stir occasionally until golden brown, about 5 minutes. Remove from oven and cool. Stir together flour, baking powder, salt and toasted coconut. Mix milk, egg, oil, sugar and vanilla together well. Add liquid mixture to dry ingredients. Stir until just blended. Pour batter into a greased, floured loaf pan (9-x-5-x-3 inches). Bake for 1 hour, or until done. Cool in pan for about 10 minutes. Turn out on a wire rack to cool completely.

SWEET POTATO BREAD

This bread is moist, spicy and irresistible.

1 cup whole wheat or all-purpose flour
1 cup all-purpose flour
1 tbs. baking powder
½ tsp. salt
1 cup sugar
¼ tsp. ground ginger
½ tsp. cinnamon

¼ tsp. nutmeg
½ cup chopped pecans or walnuts
½ cup orange juice
1 egg
⅓ cup vegetable oil
1 can (16 oz.) sweet potatoes or yams,
    drained and mashed (1⅓ cups)

Preheat oven to 350°. Combine flours, baking powder, salt, sugar, ginger, cinnamon, nutmeg and nuts. Mix orange juice, egg, oil and sweet potatoes together well. Add liquid mixture to dry ingredients. Stir until just blended. Pour batter into a greased, floured loaf pan (9-x-5-x-3 inches). Bake for 1 hour and 15 minutes, or until bread tests done. Cool in pan for about 10 minutes. Turn out on a wire rack to cool completely.

FAVORITE *QUICK MIX* BREADS

*Find your favorite flavor on the chart that follows and bake a delicious **Quick Mix** loaf. With **Quick Mix** on hand (see page 7), you can prepare one or more loaves in no time, by following these basic directions:*

1. Combine the dry ingredients.
2. Mix the liquid ingredients together well.
3. Add liquid mixture to dry ingredients. Stir until just blended.
4. Pour batter into a greased, floured loaf pan (9-x-5-x-3 inches).
5. Bake in a preheated 350° oven for 55 to 65 minutes, or until bread tests done. Or, bake in 3 small loaf pans (6-x-3-x-2 inches) for 45 to 50 minutes.
6. Cool in pans for about 10 minutes. Turn out on a wire rack to cool completely.

Be creative with basic recipes. Add an unusual spice, like cardamom or anise. Combine various nuts, fruits and vegetables. Use either honey or sugar; we have included amounts for both.

	ALMOND	APPLE	APRICOT	BANANA
QUICK MIX	3½ cups	3½ cups	3½ cups	3½ cups
Spices and Flavorings	1 tsp. almond extract	1 tsp. cinnamon		
Nuts	1 cup sliced almonds	1 cup chopped nuts	1 cup chopped nuts	1 cup chopped nuts
Variation		1 cup shredded apple	1 cup diced dried apricots	1 cup mashed banana
Egg	1	1	1	1
Honey and Liquid **OR** **Sugar and Liquid**	⅔ cup honey and 1 cup milk OR ¾ cup sugar and 1¼ cups milk	⅔ cup honey and ⅔ cup milk or apple juice OR ¾ cup brown sugar, packed, and 1 cup milk or apple juice	¾ cup honey and ¾ cup apricot nectar OR 1 cup sugar and 1 cup apricot nectar	⅔ cup honey and ⅓ cup milk OR ¾ cup sugar and ½ cup milk

	BLUEBERRY	**BUTTERSCOTCH CHIP**	**CARROT**	**CHOCOLATE OR CAROB CHIP**
QUICK MIX	3½ cups	3½ cups	3½ cups	3½ cups
Spices and Flavorings	1 tsp. grated orange peel	1 tsp. vanilla extract	1 tsp. cinnamon	
Nuts	1 cup chopped nuts	1 cup chopped nuts	1 cup chopped nuts	1 cup chopped nuts
Variation	1 cup blueberries	1 cup butterscotch chips	1 cup grated carrot	1 cup chocolate or carob chips
Egg	1	1	1	1
Honey and Liquid **OR** **Sugar and Liquid**	⅔ cup honey and 1 cup orange juice OR ¾ cup sugar and 1 cup orange juice	⅔ cup honey and 1 cup milk OR ¾ cup brown sugar, firmly packed, and 1¼ cups milk	⅔ cup honey and ⅔ cup milk OR ¾ cup brown sugar, firmly packed, and 1 cup milk	⅔ cup honey and 1 cup milk OR ¾ cup sugar and 1¼ cups milk

	COCONUT	CRANBERRY	DATE	FIG
QUICK MIX	3½ cups	3½ cups	3½ cups	3½ cups
Spices and Flavorings		1 tsp. grated orange peel	1 tsp. grated orange peel	½ tsp. cinnamon ½ tsp. allspice
Nuts	1 cup chopped nuts	1 cup chopped nuts	1 cup chopped nuts	1 cup chopped nuts
Variation	¾ cup coconut	¾ cup chopped cranberries	1 cup chopped dates	1 cup chopped dried figs
Egg	1	1	1	1
Honey and Liquid **OR** **Sugar and Liquid**	⅔ cup honey and 1 cup milk OR ¾ cup brown sugar, firmly packed, and 1¼ cups milk	⅔ cup honey and ¾ cup orange juice OR ¾ cup brown sugar, firmly packed, and 1 cup orange juice	⅔ cup honey and ¾ cup orange juice OR ¾ cup sugar and 1 cup orange juice	⅔ cup honey and ¾ cup orange juice OR ¾ cup sugar and 1 cup orange juice

	GRANOLA	LEMON	ORANGE	PEACH
QUICK MIX	3½ cups	3½ cups	3½ cups	3½ cups
Spices and Flavorings		2 tbs. grated lemon peel	2 tbs. grated orange peel	1 tsp. cinnamon
Nuts		1 cup chopped nuts	1 cup chopped nuts	1 cup chopped nuts
Variation	1 cup granola			1 cup diced dried peaches
Egg	1	1	1	1
Honey and Liquid **OR** **Sugar and Liquid**	⅔ cup honey and 1 cup milk, apple or orange juice OR ¾ cup sugar and 1¼ cups milk, apple or orange juice	⅔ cup honey and 1 cup milk OR ¾ cup sugar and 1¼ cups milk	⅔ cup honey and 1 cup orange juice OR ¾ cup sugar and 1¼ cups orange juice	⅔ cup honey and ¾ cup orange juice OR ¾ cup sugar and 1 cup orange juice

	PEANUT	PEAR	PECAN	PINEAPPLE
QUICK MIX	3½ cups	3½ cups	3½ cups	3½ cups
Spices and Flavorings		1 tsp. cinnamon		1 tbs. grated orange peel
Nuts	1 cup chopped peanuts	1 cup chopped nuts	1 cup chopped pecans	1 cup chopped nuts
Variation		1 cup diced dried pears		⅔ cup drained crushed pineapple
Egg	1	1	1	1
Honey and Liquid **OR** **Sugar and Liquid**	⅔ cup honey and 1 cup milk OR ¾ cup brown sugar, firmly packed, and 1¼ cups milk	⅔ cup honey and ¾ cup orange juice OR ¾ cup sugar and 1 cup orange juice	⅔ cup honey and 1 cup milk OR ¾ cup brown sugar, firmly packed, and 1¼ cups milk	⅔ cup honey and ⅔ cup orange juice OR ¾ cup brown sugar, firmly packed, and ¾ cup orange juice

	PRUNE	PUMPKIN	RAISIN	SPICE
QUICK MIX	3½ cups	3½ cups	3½ cups	3½ cups
Spices and Flavorings	1 tbs. grated orange peel	1 tsp. cinnamon ½ tsp. allspice		½ tsp. cinnamon ½ tsp. nutmeg ¼ tsp. ground cloves
Nuts	1 cup chopped nuts	1 cup chopped nuts	1 cup chopped nuts	1 cup chopped nuts
Variation	1 cup chopped dried prunes	1 cup canned pumpkin	1 cup raisins	
Egg	1	1	1	1
Honey and Liquid **OR** **Sugar and Liquid**	⅔ cup honey and ¾ cup prune juice OR ¾ cup sugar and 1 cup prune juice	⅔ cup honey and ⅓ cup milk OR ¾ cup sugar and ½ cup milk	⅔ cup honey and ¾ cup milk or orange juice OR ¾ cup sugar and 1 cup milk or orange juice	⅔ cup honey and 1 cup milk OR ¾ cup sugar and 1¼ cups milk

	SWEET POTATO OR YAM	**WALNUT**	**YOGURT**	**ZUCCHINI**
QUICK MIX	3½ cups	3½ cups	3½ cups	3½ cups
Spices and Flavorings	1 tsp. cinnamon ½ tsp. allspice		½ tsp. baking soda	1 tsp. cinnamon
Nuts	1 cup chopped nuts	1 cup chopped walnuts	1 cup chopped nuts	1 cup chopped nuts
Variation	1 cup mashed, cooked sweet potato or yam		1 cup yogurt, any flavor	1 cup shredded zucchini
Egg	1	1	1	1
Honey and Liquid **OR** **Sugar and Liquid**	⅔ cup honey and ⅓ cup milk OR ¾ cup sugar and ½ cup milk	⅔ cup honey and 1 cup milk OR ¾ cup sugar and 1¼ cups milk	⅔ cup honey and ½ cup milk OR ¾ cup sugar and ⅔ cup milk	⅔ cup honey and ⅔ cup milk OR ¾ cup brown sugar, packed, and 1 cup milk

BISCUITS AND SPECIAL BISCUIT BREADS

MAKING THE PERFECT BISCUIT

No packaged baking mix can rival the flavor of homemade, fresh-baked biscuits and biscuit-type breads, such as scones, shortcake and pinwheels. Here are a few hints that will help you produce delicious biscuits:

- Use chilled butter or margarine.
- Cut the butter or margarine into the dry ingredients, using a pastry blender or two knives, until the mixture resembles coarse cornmeal.
- When adding liquid to the dry ingredients, stir with a fork only until the mixture is moistened.
- To knead the dough, turn the mixture onto a floured surface. Grasp the dough with both hands and gently push it away from you with the heels of your hands. Repeat this procedure 10 to 12 times.
- Roll or pat the dough ½-inch thick, or ¼-inch thick and fold over. Cut with a 2½-inch biscuit cutter.
- To make biscuits with soft sides, place them close together on a baking sheet. If crisp biscuits are preferred, place them 2 inches apart.
- For a browner crust, brush tops of biscuits with milk before baking.

QUICK MIX BISCUITS

Makes 10

Just mix, bake and serve. Since these are so easy to put together, why not take a few minutes and add one of the variations on page 76?

2½ cups *All-Purpose or Buttermilk Quick Mix*, page 7
½ cup milk

Preheat oven to 450°. Combine *Quick Mix* and milk. Knead gently 12 times. Roll or pat dough ½-inch thick, or ¼-inch thick and fold over. Cut into squares, or 2½-inch rounds. Bake on an ungreased baking sheet for 12 minutes, or until golden brown.

For Drop Biscuits, decrease *Quick Mix* to 2 cups and combine with milk. Drop by tablespoonfuls onto a greased baking sheet. Bake for 10 to 12 minutes, or until golden brown.

BAKING POWDER BISCUITS

Enjoy these mouth-watering biscuits hot from the oven.

1 cup whole wheat or all-purpose flour
1 cup all-purpose flour
1 tbs. baking powder
½ tsp. salt
⅓ cup butter or margarine
¾ cup milk

Preheat oven to 450°. Stir together flours, baking powder and salt. Cut butter into dry ingredients until mixture resembles coarse cornmeal. Add milk and stir slightly. Knead gently 12 times. Roll or pat dough ½-inch thick or roll ¼-inch thick and fold over. Cut into squares, 2½-inch rounds or other interesting shapes with cookie cutters. Bake on an ungreased baking sheet for 12 minutes, or until golden brown.

BUTTERMILK BISCUITS

Buttermilk gives biscuits a lighter texture and distinctive flavor.

1 cup whole wheat or all-purpose flour
1 cup all-purpose flour
1 tbs. baking powder
½ tsp. baking soda
½ tsp. salt
⅓ cup butter or margarine
¾ cup buttermilk

Preheat oven to 400°. Stir together flours, baking powder, baking soda and salt. Cut butter into dry ingredients until mixture resembles coarse cornmeal. Add buttermilk and stir slightly. Knead gently 12 times. Roll or pat dough ½-inch thick or roll ¼-inch thick and fold over. Cut into squares, 2½-inch rounds or other interesting shapes with cookie cutters. Bake on an ungreased baking sheet for 12 minutes, or until golden brown.

BISCUIT VARIATIONS

*Add one of the following to the dry ingredients called for in **Quick Mix Biscuits**, page 73, **Baking Powder Biscuits**, page 74, or **Buttermilk Biscuits**, page 75.*

- ¼ tsp. dried thyme, basil or marjoram
- 2 tsp. poppy, sesame or caraway seeds
- 3 tbs. grated onion
- ½ cup grated cheese
- ½ cup chopped nuts
- ½ cup chopped dates or raisins

- **Sweet Buns**. Dip a sugar cube in orange juice and press into biscuit center.
- **Drop Biscuits**. Increase the milk to 1 cup. Drop batter by tablespoonfuls onto a greased baking sheet. Add any one of the variations to the dry ingredients.
- **Filled Biscuits**. Roll dough ¼-inch thick. Spread half of dough with any variation or jam; fold the other half over. Cut in squares or triangles.
- **Sour Cream Biscuits**. Substitute 1 cup sour cream for the milk and add ½ tsp. baking soda.

- **Pinwheel Biscuits**. Roll the dough into a 10-x-16-inch rectangle, 1/4-inch thick. Brush with about 1/3 cup melted butter or margarine and spread with any of the following fillings. Roll jelly roll style, beginning on the long edge. Cut into 1-inch slices and bake. Makes 16.

Pinwheel Fillings

- 1 cup grated cheese and 1/4 cup sliced ripe olives or sliced green onions
- 1/2 cup sugar combined with 1 tsp. cinnamon
- 1/2 cup brown sugar, firmly packed, and 1/2 cup chopped pecans or walnuts
- 1/2 cup jam or marmalade
- 1/2 cup sugar, 1 tbs. grated orange rind (zest) and 1/3 cup currants

CORNMEAL BISCUITS

Bring the feeling of a country home-style meal to your table with these biscuits.

¾ cup whole wheat or all-purpose flour
¾ cup all-purpose flour
½ cup yellow cornmeal
2 tsp. baking powder
½ tsp. baking soda
½ tsp. salt
⅓ cup butter or margarine
1 cup sour cream
1 tbs. honey or sugar
paprika, optional

Preheat oven to 450°. Stir together flours, cornmeal, baking powder, baking soda and salt. Cut butter into mixture until it resembles coarse cornmeal. Add sour cream and honey. Stir slightly. Knead 12 times. Roll or pat dough ½-inch thick, or ¼-inch thick and fold over. Cut into 2½-inch rounds. If desired, sprinkle with paprika. Bake on an ungreased baking sheet for 10 minutes, or until golden brown.

RYE BISCUITS

Make little rye biscuit sandwiches to serve with soup.

1 cup all-purpose flour
1 cup rye flour
1 tbs. baking powder
½ tsp. baking soda
½ tsp. salt
1 tbs. caraway seeds
⅓ cup butter or margarine
¾ cup buttermilk

Preheat oven to 425°. Stir together flours, baking powder, baking soda, salt and caraway seeds. Cut butter into dry ingredients until mixture resembles coarse cornmeal. Add buttermilk and stir slightly. Knead dough gently 12 times. Roll or pat dough ½-inch thick, or ¼-inch thick and fold over. Cut into squares or 2½-inch rounds. Bake on an ungreased baking sheet for 12 minutes, or until done.

SWEET BISCUITS

Begin the day with hot biscuits fresh from the oven.

2 cups all-purpose flour
1 tbs. baking powder
1/2 tsp. salt
1/2 cup butter or margarine
3/4 cup cream
1 tbs. honey
1/4 cup milk
2 tbs. sugar

Preheat oven to 450°. Stir together flour, baking powder and salt. Cut butter into dry ingredients until mixture resembles coarse cornmeal. Add cream and honey. Stir until blended. Knead gently 12 times. Roll or pat dough 1/2-inch thick, or 1/4-inch thick and fold over. Cut into 2 1/2-inch rounds. Brush with milk and sprinkle with sugar. Bake on an ungreased baking sheet for 12 minutes, or until golden brown.

SWEET POTATO BISCUITS

This biscuit complements a turkey or ham dinner.

¾ cup whole wheat or all-purpose flour
¾ cup all-purpose flour
2½ tsp. baking powder
½ tsp. salt
1 tbs. brown sugar, firmly packed
⅓ cup butter or margarine
¼ cup milk
½ cup cooked or canned sweet potato, mashed
1 tsp. cinnamon, optional

Preheat oven to 425°. Stir together flours, baking powder, salt and brown sugar. Cut butter into dry ingredients until mixture resembles coarse cornmeal. Stir in milk and sweet potato. Knead gently 12 times. Roll or pat dough ½-inch thick, or ¼-inch thick and fold over. Cut into 2½-inch rounds. If desired, sprinkle with cinnamon. Bake on an ungreased baking sheet for 10 to 12 minutes, or until done.

ENERGY-PACKED DROP BISCUITS

Makes 16

Healthful ingredients have been added to make a nutritious snack.

1 cup all-purpose flour
½ cup soy flour
⅓ cup wheat germ
2 tbs. unprocessed bran
⅓ cup instant nonfat dry milk
1 tbs. baking powder
½ tsp. baking soda
¼ tsp. salt
⅓ cup butter or margarine

¼ cup chopped dates or raisins
¼ cup chopped nuts or sunflower seed
  kernels
½ cup plain yogurt
2 tbs. molasses
2 tbs. honey
¼ cup orange juice

Preheat oven to 400°. Stir together flours, wheat germ, bran, dry milk, baking powder, baking soda and salt. Cut butter into dry ingredients until mixture resembles coarse cornmeal. Add chopped dates and nuts. Mix yogurt, molasses, honey and orange juice together well. Add liquid mixture to dry ingredients. Stir slightly until moistened. Drop by tablespoonfuls onto a greased baking sheet. Bake for 10 minutes, or until golden brown.

HERB CHEESE DROP BISCUITS

Makes 6 large or 12 regular size

*For a light meal, split these biscuits and top them with **Ratatouille**, page 147.*

2 cups *All-Purpose or Buttermilk Quick Mix*, page 7
1/4 tsp. dried dill weed
1/4 tsp. dried oregano
3/4 cup grated cheddar cheese
3/4 cup milk

Preheat oven to 450°. Stir together *Quick Mix*, dill, oregano and cheese. Add milk and stir until moistened. Divide into 6 large drop biscuits. Bake on a greased baking sheet for 15 minutes, or until golden brown.

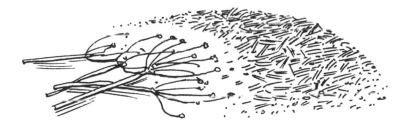

SESAME SEED DROP BISCUITS

The sesame seeds add to the delicious flavor of this wholesome biscuit.

1½ cups whole wheat flour
½ cup wheat germ
1 tbs. baking powder
½ tsp. baking soda
½ tsp. salt
⅓ cup butter or margarine
1 egg
1 cup buttermilk
1 tbs. honey or sugar
¼ cup butter or margarine, melted
½ cup sesame seeds

Preheat oven to 400°. Mix flour, wheat germ, baking powder, baking soda and salt together. Cut in butter until mixture resembles coarse cornmeal. Combine egg, buttermilk and honey. Stir liquid mixture into dry ingredients. Drop by tablespoonfuls onto a greased baking sheet. Brush with melted butter and sprinkle with sesame seeds. Bake for 12 to 15 minutes.

BREADSTICKS

Fresh breadsticks are just right with soup and salad.

2 cups all-purpose flour
1 tbs. baking powder
1/2 tsp. salt
1/4 cup butter or margarine
2 eggs
1/2 cup milk
1/4 cup butter or margarine, melted
2 tbs. sesame seeds, optional

Preheat oven to 450°. Stir together flour, baking powder and salt. Cut unmelted butter into dry ingredients until mixture resembles coarse cornmeal. Mix together eggs and milk. Stir liquid mixture into dry ingredients until moistened. Roll or pat dough into an 8-x-6-inch rectangle, 1/2-inch thick. Cut into sticks, each 4 inches long and 1/2-inch wide. Roll gently to round the sides. Sprinkle with flour if dough is too sticky to handle easily. Brush a cookie sheet with 1 tbs. of the melted butter. Place breadsticks on sheet and brush with remaining melted butter. If desired, sprinkle with sesame seeds. Bake for 12 minutes, or until golden brown.

CHEESE CORNSTICKS

Serve these richly flavored cornsticks at your next barbecue.

1 cup all-purpose flour
¾ cup cornmeal
1 tbs. baking powder
½ tsp. baking soda
½ tsp. salt
½ cup shredded cheddar or Monterey Jack cheese
¼ cup honey or sugar
1 cup sour cream
1 egg
2 tbs. vegetable oil

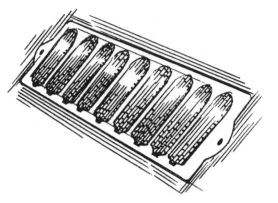

Preheat oven to 425°. Stir together flour, cornmeal, baking powder, baking soda, salt and cheese. Mix honey, sour cream, egg and oil together well. Add liquid mixture to dry ingredients. Stir until just blended. Rest batter for 5 minutes. Grease a cornstick pan, and fill each section ⅔ full. Bake for 12 to 15 minutes, or until golden brown.

SHORTCAKE

Top with any fresh fruit in season and add a dollop of whipped cream, whipped topping or even yogurt.

1 cup whole wheat or all-purpose flour
1 cup all-purpose flour
1 tbs. baking powder
½ tsp. salt
½ cup butter or margarine

⅔ cup light cream
1 egg
2 tbs. honey or sugar
1 tbs. sugar

Preheat oven to 450°. Mix flours, baking powder and salt together. Cut butter into dry ingredients until mixture resembles coarse cornmeal. Stir cream, egg and honey together well. Add liquid mixture to dry ingredients. Stir until moistened. Pat dough into a greased, floured 8-x-8-x-2-inch square pan or an 8-x-1½-inch round pan and sprinkle with sugar. Bake for 15 minutes, or until golden brown. Serve warm, split and filled with fruit and topping.

For individual shortcakes prepare shortcake dough. Knead dough gently on a floured surface, then pat or roll ½-inch thick. Cut 8 shortcakes with a 2½-inch round cutter. Sprinkle with sugar. Bake for 8 to 10 minutes on an ungreased baking sheet.

SCONES

Scones are a British tradition and can be cut into a variety of shapes — squares, diamonds, hearts or triangles. Serve hot from the oven with butter and jam.

1 cup whole wheat or all-purpose flour
1 cup all-purpose flour
1 tbs. baking powder
1/2 tsp. salt
6 tbs. butter or margarine
1/2 cup milk
1 egg
2 tbs. honey or sugar

Preheat oven to 425°. Mix together flours, baking powder and salt. Cut butter into dry ingredients until mixture resembles coarse cornmeal. Combine milk, egg and honey. Stir liquid mixture into dry ingredients until moistened. Knead 15 times on a floured surface. Divide dough in half and form into 2 balls. Roll or pat each ball 1/2-inch thick, forming two 6-inch circles. Cut each circle into 6 wedges. Or pat the dough 1/2-inch thick and cut into squares, triangles or diamonds. Bake on an ungreased baking sheet for 12 minutes or until golden brown.

VARIATIONS

- Add ½ cup dried currants, raisins, dried cranberries, dried cherries or chopped nuts to dry ingredients.
- Use buttermilk in place of milk and add ½ tsp. baking soda.
- Roll the dough ¼-inch thick, fold it over once and cut it into triangles. Brush the top with egg white and sprinkle with sugar before baking.

RAISIN NUT PINWHEELS

Makes 12

A plate of these delightful treats will disappear quickly!

2 cups *All-Purpose or Buttermilk Quick Mix*, page 7
1/4 tsp. baking soda
1/2 cup raisins

1/2 cup sour cream
1/4 cup milk
1/4 cup butter, melted
Filling, follows

Preheat oven to 450°. Stir together *Quick Mix*, baking soda and raisins. Mix together sour cream and milk. Stir into dry ingredients. Knead gently 12 times. Roll dough to a 1/4-inch-thick rectangle of about 10-x-12 inches. Brush with melted butter. Sprinkle filling over dough. Roll jelly roll style, beginning at the long edge. Seal ends. Cut into 1-inch slices. Place on an ungreased baking sheet. Bake for 12 minutes, or until golden brown.

FILLING

1/4 cup brown sugar, firmly packed
2 tbs. wheat germ

1/4 cup chopped pecans or walnuts
1/2 tsp. cinnamon

Combine filling ingredients.

QUICK MIX HOT CROSS BUNS

Hot cross buns are traditionally served for Easter, but are also a special treat on other occasions.

2 cups *All-Purpose or Buttermilk Quick Mix*, page 7
1/4 cup currants or raisins
1/4 cup mixed candied fruit
1 tsp. cinnamon
1 tsp. instant coffee powder

1/4 cup sugar
1/2 cup milk
1 egg yolk
1 tbs. water
Frosting, follows

Preheat oven to 450°. Stir together *Quick Mix*, currants, candied fruit, cinnamon, coffee powder and sugar. Add milk and stir to form a soft dough. Knead on a floured surface 25 times. Shape into 8 balls and place close together in a greased, floured 8-inch round baking pan. Combine egg yolk and water. Brush over tops of buns. Bake for 15 minutes, or until golden brown. Cool and drizzle frosting over each bun to form an X.

FROSTING
1/3 cup confectioners' sugar

1 tsp. milk

Combine ingredients.

RIESKA BREAD

Barbara's grandmother, Hannah, baked this traditional Finnish flatbread often for her family.

1½ cups all-purpose flour
¾ cup barley flour
1½ tsp. baking powder
½ tsp. baking soda
½ tsp. salt
2 tbs. sugar
¼ cup butter or margarine
1 cup buttermilk

Preheat oven to 425°. Stir together flours, baking powder, baking soda, salt and sugar. Cut butter into dry ingredients until mixture resembles coarse cornmeal. Stir in buttermilk until a soft dough is formed. Roll or pat dough on a greased cookie sheet into a 10-inch circle. Bake for 20 minutes, or until golden brown. Cut with a serrated knife.

IRISH OATMEAL SODA BREAD

It's not just for the Irish — this classic bread is enjoyed by all.

1½ cups all-purpose flour
½ cup quick-cooking oats
2½ tsp. baking powder
½ tsp. baking soda
½ tsp. salt

2 tsp. caraway seeds
1 tbs. sugar
⅓ cup butter or margarine
½ cup currants or raisins
¾ cup buttermilk

Preheat oven to 375°. Stir together flour, oats, baking powder, baking soda, salt, caraway seeds and sugar. Cut butter into dry ingredients until mixture resembles coarse cornmeal. Stir in currants. Add buttermilk and stir until blended. Knead gently 12 times. Shape dough into a 7-inch circle on an ungreased baking sheet. Cut a large X about ¼-inch deep across top of entire circle of dough. Bake for 30 minutes, or until golden brown. Cut into wedges to serve.

SCRUMPTIOUS COFFEECAKES

MAKING THE PERFECT COFFEECAKE

Here are a few suggestions for making perfect coffeecakes every time:

- If the recipe calls for butter or margarine, allow it to soften at room temperature. Then beat it until it becomes creamy.
- When adding dry ingredients to a creamed mixture alternately with the liquid ingredients, be sure not to overmix.
- Coffeecake is done when a toothpick inserted into the middle comes out clean. It will also start to pull away from the sides of the pan. Don't overbake.
- Make early morning minutes count by doing most of the preliminary preparation the night before: Measure the *Quick Mix* or dry ingredients into a bowl. Combine the milk, eggs and honey (liquid ingredients) and refrigerate. Mix the topping ingredients and set aside. All you have to do in the morning is preheat the oven, mix the batter and sprinkle on the topping. Less than 5 minutes will do it!

The same preparation steps will work for many of the quick bread recipes in this book. It is an especially handy technique when preparing for guests.

QUICK MIX COFFEECAKE

Makes 9 servings

Wake up your "sleepy heads" with the heavenly aroma of coffeecake baking in the oven. It's possible, even on busy mornings, by using this Quick Mix recipe. There are 5 different toppings to choose from on pages 98 and 99.

½ cup milk
1 egg
⅓ cup honey or sugar
2 cups *All-Purpose* or *Buttermilk Quick Mix*, page 7

Preheat oven to 400°. Combine milk, egg and honey. Add to *Quick Mix*. Stir until just blended. Pour batter into a greased, floured baking pan (8-x-8-x-2 inches). Spread with desired topping and bake for 20 minutes, or until done.

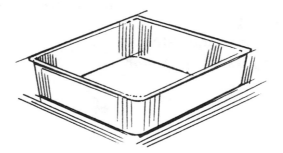

BASIC COFFEECAKE

Five different coffeecakes can be made from this basic recipe. Choose your favorite topping on pages 98 and 99.

½ cup butter or margarine, softened
½ cup honey or sugar
1 egg
2 cups all-purpose flour
1 tbs. baking powder
½ tsp. salt
1 tbs. grated lemon or orange rind (zest), optional
⅔ cup milk when using honey (¾ cup milk when using sugar)
½ tsp. vanilla extract

Preheat oven to 400°. Cream butter and honey. Mix in egg. Stir together flour, baking powder, salt and lemon zest. Add dry ingredients to creamed mixture alternately with milk and vanilla. Pour batter into a greased, floured baking pan (9-x-9-x-2 inches). Spread desired topping over batter. Bake for 25 to 30 minutes, or until cake tests done.

COFFEECAKE TOPPINGS

First combine the dry ingredients. Cut the butter or margarine into the dry ingredients until the mixture is crumbly. Sprinkle evenly over the coffeecake batter and bake as directed in coffeecake recipes.

GRANOLA TOPPING
1 cup granola
1/3 cup brown sugar, firmly packed

1/2 tsp. cinnamon
3 tbs. butter or margarine, softened

COCONUT TOPPING
1 cup shredded coconut
1/2 cup chopped pecans or walnuts

1/3 cup brown sugar, firmly packed
1/4 cup butter or margarine, softened

PECAN WHEAT GERM TOPPING
1/2 cup chopped pecans
1/2 cup wheat germ

1/3 cup brown sugar, firmly packed
1/4 cup butter or margarine, softened

CINNAMON SUGAR TOPPING

3 tbs. whole wheat or all-purpose flour
1/3 cup brown sugar, firmly packed
1/2 cup chopped pecans or walnuts

1 tsp. cinnamon
1/4 cup butter or margarine, softened

APPLE CHEESE TOPPING

Arrange 1 cup peeled, thinly sliced apples on top of batter, and sprinkle evenly with this crumbled mixture:

1/2 cup quick cooking oats
1/2 cup shredded cheddar cheese

1/3 cup brown sugar, firmly packed
1/4 cup butter or margarine, softened

APPLE GRAHAM COFFEECAKE

Makes 9 servings

Graham cracker crumbs, shredded apples, cinnamon and nuts give this coffee-cake a distinctive flavor.

¼ cup butter or margarine, softened
½ cup brown sugar, firmly packed
1 egg
1 cup graham cracker crumbs
1 cup all-purpose flour
2 tsp. baking powder
½ tsp. baking soda

¼ tsp. salt
½ tsp. allspice
1 tsp. cinnamon
¼ cup chopped almonds or walnuts
1 cup shredded peeled apple
¼ cup milk
confectioners' sugar, optional

Preheat oven to 375°. Cream butter and sugar. Mix in egg. Stir together graham cracker crumbs, flour, baking powder, baking soda, salt, allspice, cinnamon and nuts. Stir dry ingredients into creamed mixture alternately with apple and milk. Spread batter into a greased, floured baking pan (8-x-8-x-2 inches). Bake for 35 minutes, or until cake tests done. Cool and dust with confectioners' sugar.

AVOCADO ORANGE COFFEECAKE

The unusual addition of the avocado, combined with the orange juice, creates a special flavor we think you'll really like.

2 cups all-purpose flour
¾ cup brown sugar, firmly packed
1 tbs. baking powder
½ tsp. salt
1 tsp. cinnamon
½ cup chopped pecans or walnuts

¾ cup mashed avocado
¼ cup vegetable oil
1 egg
¾ cup orange juice
Orange Glaze, follows

Preheat oven to 400°. Stir together flour, brown sugar, baking powder, salt, cinnamon and nuts. Mix avocado, oil, egg and orange juice together well. Add liquid mixture to dry ingredients. Stir until just blended. Spread batter into a greased, floured baking pan (9-x-9-x-2 inches). Bake for 30 minutes, or until cake tests done, and spread *Orange Glaze* over warm cake.

ORANGE GLAZE

½ cup confectioners' sugar
1 tsp. grated orange rind (zest)

1 tbs. orange juice

Combine ingredients.

FABULOUS BEER COFFEECAKE

Makes 10-12 servings

This is another unusual, and absolutely delicious, coffeecake.

1 cup butter or margarine, softened
1½ cups brown sugar, firmly packed
2 eggs
3 cups all-purpose flour
2 tsp. baking soda
½ tsp. salt
1 tsp. cinnamon

½ tsp. allspice
½ tsp. ground cloves
1 cup chopped walnuts
2 cups chopped dates
1 can (12 oz.) beer
Lemon Glaze, follows

Preheat oven to 350°. Cream butter and sugar. Mix in eggs. Stir together flour, baking soda, salt, cinnamon, allspice, cloves, walnuts and dates. Add dry ingredients to creamed mixture alternately with beer. Pour batter into a greased, floured tube pan (10 inches). Bake for 1 hour and 15 minutes, or until cake tests done. Cool in pan for 10 minutes. Turn out on a wire rack to cool completely. Spread with *Lemon Glaze*.

LEMON GLAZE

1 cup confectioners' sugar
2 tbs. lemon juice

1 tsp. grated lemon rind (zest)

Combine ingredients.

PINEAPPLE CARROT COFFEECAKE

Here's that familiar carrot cake flavor everyone loves.

1½ cups all-purpose flour
¾ cup brown sugar, firmly packed
2½ tsp. baking powder
½ tsp. salt
1 tsp. cinnamon
1 cup shredded carrots
½ cup chopped nuts

¼ cup vegetable oil
1 egg
1 can (8 oz.) crushed pineapple with
 juice
1 tsp. vanilla extract
Cream Cheese Frosting, follows

Preheat oven to 350°. Stir together flour, brown sugar, baking powder, salt, cinnamon, carrots and nuts. Mix oil, egg, pineapple and vanilla together well. Add liquid mixture to dry ingredients. Stir until just blended. Pour batter into a greased, floured baking pan (9-x-9-x-2 inches). Bake for 40 minutes, or until cake tests done. Cool. Spread *Cream Cheese Frosting* over coffeecake.

CREAM CHEESE FROSTING

3 oz. cream cheese
3 tbs. confectioners' sugar

1 tbs. milk
½ tsp. vanilla extract

Combine ingredients until creamy.

OATMEAL COCONUT COFFEECAKE

Makes 12-15 servings

Fabulous! It makes a good addition to a lunch box.

1 cup quick-cooking oats
½ cup butter or margarine, cut into 5 slices
1⅓ cups boiling water
¾ cup sugar
¾ cup brown sugar, firmly packed
2 eggs
¾ cup whole wheat or all-purpose flour
¾ cup all-purpose flour
2 tsp. baking powder
1 tsp. baking soda
¼ tsp. salt
1 tsp. cinnamon
½ tsp. nutmeg
Coconut Topping, follows

Preheat oven to 350°. Combine oats, butter and boiling water. Let stand for 20 minutes. Beat together sugars and eggs. Stir together flours, baking powder, baking soda, salt, cinnamon and nutmeg. Add dry ingredients to sugar and eggs alternately with oats mixture. Pour batter into a greased, floured baking pan (9-x-13 inches). Bake for 35 minutes, or until cake tests done. Spread with *Coconut Topping* and broil until topping is golden brown. Serve warm.

COCONUT TOPPING
1/3 cup butter or margarine, melted
3/4 cup brown sugar, firmly packed
1/4 cup milk
1 cup coconut
1 cup chopped nuts

Combine ingredients.

CHOCOLATE CHIP COFFEECAKE

Chocolate lovers will enjoy this marvelous coffeecake.

½ cup butter or margarine, softened
¾ cup sugar
2 eggs
2 cups all-purpose flour
1 tbs. baking powder

½ tsp. salt
1 cup milk
1 tsp. vanilla extract
1 cup chocolate chips
Topping, follows

Preheat oven to 350°. Cream butter and sugar. Mix in eggs. Stir together flour, baking powder and salt. Add dry ingredients to creamed mixture alternately with milk and vanilla. Stir in chocolate chips. Spread batter into a greased, floured baking pan (9-x-9-x-2 inches). Sprinkle *Topping* over batter. Bake for 40 minutes, or until cake tests done.

TOPPING
½ cup chopped pecans or walnuts
1 tbs. sugar

Combine ingredients.

SPICED SOUR CREAM COFFEECAKE

Makes 9 servings

A favorite in Barbara's family, this recipe is perfect to freeze and have on hand for unexpected guests.

1½ cups all-purpose flour
½ cup brown sugar, firmly packed
⅓ cup granulated sugar
1 tsp. cinnamon
½ tsp. nutmeg
½ tsp. ground ginger

½ cup vegetable oil
2 tsp. baking powder
½ tsp. baking soda
½ tsp. salt
1 egg
½ cup sour cream

Preheat oven to 350°. Stir together flour, sugars and spices. Blend in oil. Set aside ½ cup of this mixture. To the remainder, add baking powder, baking soda, salt, egg and sour cream. Mix well and spread into a greased, floured baking pan (8-x-8-x-2 inches). Sprinkle reserved mixture over batter. Bake for 30 minutes, or until cake tests done.

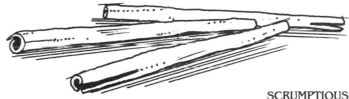

PRUNE COFFEECAKE

This recipe makes a moist cake that's perfect for a picnic.

½ cup butter or margarine, softened
1½ cups sugar
3 eggs
2 tsp. vanilla extract
2½ cups all-purpose flour
2 tsp. baking powder
1 tsp. baking soda
½ tsp. salt

1 tsp. cinnamon
1 tsp. allspice
½ tsp. ground cloves
1 cup buttermilk
1 cup chopped pecans or walnuts
1 cup chopped dried prunes
confectioners' sugar, optional

Preheat oven to 350°. Cream butter and sugar. Mix in eggs and vanilla. Stir together flour, baking powder, baking soda, salt, cinnamon, allspice and cloves. Add dry ingredients to creamed mixture alternately with buttermilk. Stir in nuts and prunes. Pour batter into a greased, floured tube pan or Bundt pan (10 inches). Bake for 65 minutes or until cake tests done. Cool in pan for 5 minutes. Turn out on wire rack to cool completely. Dust with confectioners' sugar.

PUMPKIN COFFEECAKE

Make this cake quickly and enjoy it warm from the oven.

2 cups *All-Purpose* or *Buttermilk Quick Mix*, page 7
1/2 cup brown sugar, firmly packed
1/2 tsp. cinnamon
1/4 tsp. ground ginger
1/4 tsp. ground cloves

1/2 cup raisins
1/2 cup chopped nuts
1/4 cup milk
2 eggs
3/4 cup canned pumpkin
Topping, follows

Preheat oven to 350°. Stir together *Quick Mix*, brown sugar, cinnamon, ginger, cloves, raisins and nuts. Mix milk, eggs and pumpkin together well. Add liquid ingredients to dry ingredients. Stir until just blended. Spread batter in a greased, floured baking pan (8-x-8-x-2 inches). Sprinkle *Topping* over cake batter. Bake for 40 minutes, or until cake tests done. Serve warm.

TOPPING

2 tbs. *Quick Mix*
1/4 cup brown sugar, firmly packed
1/2 tsp. cinnamon

2 tbs. chopped pecans or walnuts
2 tbs. butter or margarine

Combine dry ingredients and cut in butter until mixture is crumbly.

STREUSEL COFFEECAKE

Streusel and apple slices swirl through this rich coffeecake.

1 cup butter or margarine
1½ cups sugar
2 eggs
1½ cups whole wheat flour
1½ cups all-purpose flour

1 tbs. baking powder
½ tsp. salt
1 cup milk
Streusel, follows
1 apple, thinly sliced

STREUSEL
½ cup brown sugar
¾ cup chopped walnuts or pecans

1 tbs. cinnamon

Preheat oven to 350°. Cream butter and sugar. Mix in eggs. Stir together flours, baking powder and salt. Add to creamed mixture alternately with milk. In a small bowl, combine *Streusel* ingredients. Grease and flour a 10-inch tube pan. Spread ingredients as follows: ⅓ of the batter, ⅓ of the *Streusel*, ½ of the apple slices; ⅓ of the batter, ⅓ of the *Streusel*, ½ of the apple slices, ⅓ of the batter; top with remaining *Streusel*. Bake for 1 hour and 10 minutes or until done. Serve warm.

BLUEBERRY BUCKLE COFFEECAKE

This may become a family favorite at your house.

½ cup butter or margarine, softened
½ cup sugar
1 egg
1 cup whole wheat or all-purpose flour
1 cup all-purpose flour
2½ tsp. baking powder

½ tsp. baking soda
½ tsp. salt
⅔ cup buttermilk
2 cups blueberries
Topping, follows

Preheat oven to 375°. Cream butter and sugar. Mix in egg. Stir together flours, baking powder, baking soda and salt. Add dry ingredients to creamed mixture alternately with buttermilk. Gently stir in blueberries. Spread batter into a greased, floured baking pan (9-x-9-x-2 inches). Sprinkle with topping. Bake for 50 minutes, or until cake tests done. Serve warm.

TOPPING

½ cup sugar
⅓ cup whole wheat or all-purpose flour

½ tsp. cinnamon
¼ cup butter or margarine, softened

Combine sugar, flour and cinnamon. Cut butter into dry ingredients until crumbly.

UPSIDE DOWN COFFEECAKE

Makes 9 servings

This classic coffeecake has several variations in addition to the usual pineapple.

½ cup butter or margarine, softened
½ cup sugar
1 egg
1 cup whole wheat or all-purpose flour
1 cup all-purpose flour
1 tbs. baking powder

½ tsp. salt
⅔ cup milk
3 tbs. butter or margarine
¼ cup brown sugar, firmly packed
Topping Variations, follow

Preheat oven to 375°. Cream butter and sugar. Mix in egg. Stir together flours, baking powder and salt. Add dry ingredients to creamed mixture alternately with milk. Set aside. Melt 3 tbs. butter in a baking pan (9-x-9-x-2 inches) in oven. Sprinkle brown sugar over butter. Arrange fruit topping, cut side up, in an attractive pattern in the pan, or sprinkle with coconut and pecans. Spread batter in pan and bake for 30 to 35 minutes. Remove from oven and immediately invert pan onto a platter, but keep pan over cake for several minutes. Remove pan and serve warm.

TOPPING VARIATIONS

- 9 pineapple rings with a maraschino cherry in the center of each
- 2 cups peeled apple slices, ¼ cup raisins, ¼ cup walnut halves and ½ tsp. cinnamon
- 1 cup banana slices. Brush the cake with 3 tbs. rum before serving.
- ½ cup coconut and ½ cup pecans

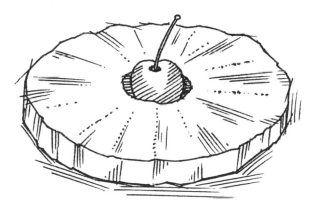

WHOLESOME COFFEECAKE

Makes 9 servings

For a nutritious snack, serve this coffeecake at any time of day.

½ cup soy flour
1 cup all-purpose flour
⅓ cup wheat germ
2 tbs. unprocessed bran
⅓ cup instant nonfat dry milk
1 tbs. baking powder
1 tsp. baking soda
¼ tsp. salt
½ cup chopped dates or raisins

½ cup chopped nuts
1 cup yogurt
1 egg
¼ cup vegetable oil
1 tbs. molasses
3 tbs. honey
2 tbs. orange juice
Topping, follows

Preheat oven to 350°. Stir together flours, wheat germ, bran, dry milk, baking powder, baking soda, salt, dates and nuts. Mix yogurt, egg, oil, molasses, honey and orange juice together well. Add liquid mixture to dry ingredients. Stir until just blended. Pour batter into a greased, floured baking pan (9-x-9-x-2 inches). Sprinkle with *Topping*. Bake for 35 minutes, or until cake tests done.

TOPPING

¼ cup wheat germ
⅓ cup date sugar or firmly packed brown sugar
¼ cup chopped pecans or walnuts
1 tsp. cinnamon
¼ cup butter or margarine, softened

Stir together wheat germ, date sugar, nuts and cinnamon. Cut butter into dry ingredients until mixture is crumbly.

GINGERBREAD

We've added a special buttermilk syrup to glaze this old favorite.

½ cup butter or margarine
½ cup dark molasses
¼ cup honey or sugar
1 egg
1 cup whole wheat or all-purpose flour
1 cup all-purpose flour
2 tsp. baking powder
1½ tsp. baking soda

½ tsp. salt
1 tsp. ground ginger
1 tsp. cinnamon
¼ tsp. nutmeg
¼ tsp. ground cloves
½ cup buttermilk
Buttermilk Glaze, follows

Preheat oven to 350°. Cream butter. Mix in molasses, honey and egg. Combine flours, baking powder, baking soda, salt, ginger, cinnamon, nutmeg and cloves. Stir into butter mixture alternately with buttermilk. Pour batter into a greased, floured baking pan (9-x-9-x-2 inches). Bake for 40 minutes or until done. Serve warm, topped with *Buttermilk Glaze*.

BUTTERMILK GLAZE

3 tbs. butter or margarine
3 tbs. honey or sugar
¼ cup buttermilk
¼ tsp. baking soda
½ tsp. vanilla extract

Combine ingredients in a small saucepan. Cook over low heat until syrupy, about 15 minutes, stirring frequently.

PERFECT PANCAKES, WAFFLES AND POPOVERS

MAKING THE PERFECT PANCAKE

- For pancakes and waffles, stir together the liquid and dry ingredients only until they are just moistened. Do not overmix. The batter will be slightly lumpy.
- For lighter pancakes or waffles, separate the egg and beat the white until stiff, but not dry. Fold beaten egg white into batter.
- It is only necessary to lightly oil the surface of the pan for the first batch of pancakes.
- Pancakes should be turned when bubbles appear and the edges are dry. Check the underside of the pancake to see if it is well browned. Pick up an edge of the pancake with a spatula and take a peek. Remember, the second side of the pancake takes less time to cook. Serve immediately.

MAKING THE PERFECT WAFFLE

- Mix the batter as you would for "the perfect pancake."
- Preheat the waffle iron to the hottest temperature possible. When a drop of water sizzles on the surface, add the batter.
- Spoon or pour the waffle batter onto the hot iron to about 1 inch from the edge. This will allow the waffle to expand and rise without spilling over the edges of the iron.

- Waffles are done when they have stopped steaming, or when they have reached the desired degree of brownness. The longer you bake waffles, the crisper they will be.

MAKING THE PERFECT POPOVER

- Beat ingredients together until smooth.
- Perfect popovers are high and light with a crisp, golden brown shell.
- Heat the popover pan, muffin cups or custard cups in the oven before filling.
- Do not open the oven while popovers are baking — they will collapse!
- Prick popovers with a fork or skewer as soon as you remove them from the oven, to release steam. Serve immediately, or they will lose their "pop."

QUICK MIX STACK

Rushing in the morning? Make Quick Mix pancakes! Serve them hot with butter, syrup, honey or jam.

2 cups *All-Purpose or Buttermilk Quick Mix,* page 7
1 tbs. sugar or honey
1 egg
1¼ cups milk

Stir together *Quick Mix* and sugar. Mix egg and milk together well. Add liquid mixture to dry ingredients. Stir only until moistened. If thinner pancakes are desired, add more milk. Pour or spoon batter onto a hot griddle or skillet. Cook on both sides until golden brown.

MELT-IN-YOUR-MOUTH PANCAKES

Watch your family's eyes light up when these are served!

¾ cup whole wheat or all-purpose flour
¾ cup all-purpose flour
2½ tsp. baking powder
½ tsp. salt
1 tbs. sugar or honey
1 egg
1¼ cups milk
3 tbs. butter or margarine, melted, or vegetable oil

Stir together flours, baking powder, salt and sugar. Mix egg, milk and butter together well. Add this mixture to dry ingredients. Stir only until moistened. If thinner pancakes are desired, add more milk. Pour or spoon batter onto a hot griddle or skillet. Cook on both sides until golden brown.

PANCAKE VARIATIONS

Add any one of the following ingredients or changes to a basic pancake batter.

- replace milk with buttermilk and add ½ tsp. baking soda
- ½ cup chopped dates
- ¾ cup blueberries
- ½ cup chopped pecans or walnuts
- substitute ½ cup quick-cooking oats for ½ cup flour
- ½ cup chopped peaches
- ½ cup shredded apple and ⅛ tsp. cinnamon
- ½ cup chopped banana and 1 tbs. grated orange rind (zest)

BUTTERMILK PANCAKES

Barbara's father, Bob, picked wild blueberries in northern Minnesota for his family's favorite pancakes.

2 cups all-purpose flour
1 tsp. baking soda
½ tsp. salt
2 cups buttermilk
3 eggs, separated
¼ cup butter or margarine, melted
1 cup blueberries, optional

Stir together flour, baking soda and salt. Combine buttermilk, egg yolks and melted butter. Add liquid mixture to dry ingredients. Stir until just moistened. Beat egg whites until stiff and fold into batter. Gently fold in blueberries, if desired. Pour or spoon batter onto a hot griddle or skillet. Cook on both sides until golden brown.

BUCKWHEAT PANCAKES

Here are perfect pancakes for mountain fishing trips and other camping trips.

1½ cups whole wheat flour
½ cup buckwheat flour
1 tbs. baking powder
½ tsp. salt
2 cups milk
½ cup vegetable oil
2 tbs. molasses, optional
3 eggs, separated

Stir together whole wheat flour, buckwheat flour, baking powder and salt. Mix milk, oil, molasses and egg yolks together well. Add liquid mixture to dry ingredients. Stir just until moistened. Beat egg whites until stiff and fold into batter. Pour or spoon batter onto a hot griddle or skillet. Cook on both sides until golden brown.

SOUR CREAM PANCAKES

This rich, satisfying pancakes are ideal for special occasions.

1 cup whole wheat flour
1/2 cup wheat germ
2 tbs. unprocessed bran
1 1/2 tsp. baking powder
1/4 tsp. baking soda
1/2 tsp. salt
1/2 cup sour cream
1 egg, separated
2 tbs. honey or molasses
1 1/4 cups milk
3 tbs. butter or margarine, melted, or vegetable oil

Stir together flour, wheat germ, bran, baking powder, baking soda and salt. Mix sour cream, egg yolk, honey, milk and butter together well. Add liquid mixture to dry ingredients. Stir until just moistened. Beat egg white until stiff and fold into batter. Pour or spoon batter onto a hot griddle or skillet. Cook on both sides until golden brown.

NUTRITION-PACKED PANCAKES

Makes 10-12 medium

When you're looking for a breakfast that's good for you, choose these pancakes instead of eggs and bacon. Since soy flour browns quickly, we suggest that you keep a close watch as they cook, to avoid burning.

½ cup soy flour
½ cup whole wheat or all-purpose flour
½ cup all-purpose flour
2 tbs. wheat germ
2 tbs. unprocessed bran
2 tbs. instant nonfat dry milk
1 tbs. baking powder
½ tsp. baking soda

¼ tsp. salt
2 tsp. grated orange rind (zest)
½ cup yogurt
2 eggs, separated
3 tbs. vegetable oil
1 tbs. molasses or honey
1 cup orange juice

Stir together flours, wheat germ, bran, instant milk, baking powder, baking soda, salt and orange zest. Mix yogurt, egg yolks, oil, molasses and orange juice together well. Add liquid mixture to dry ingredients. Stir until just moistened. Beat egg whites until stiff and fold into batter. Pour or spoon batter onto a moderately hot griddle or skillet, about 350°. Cook on both sides until golden brown.

OVEN PANCAKE

This light, delicious pancake puffs high. It is traditionally served with fruit, but it is also excellent with maple or fruit syrup.

½ cup all-purpose flour
¼ tsp. salt
1 tbs. sugar
3 eggs
½ cup milk
2 tbs. butter or margarine, melted

Preheat oven to 425°. Stir together flour, salt and sugar. Mix eggs, milk and melted butter together well. Add liquid mixture to dry ingredients. Mix until smooth. Oil a 10-inch oven-safe skillet or pie pan and pour batter into pan. Bake for 15 minutes. Reduce heat to 350° and bake for 5 to 10 additional minutes or until golden brown. Remove from oven and cut into wedges. Serve immediately.

VARIATIONS

- Squeeze a wedge of fresh lemon over baked pancake and dust with confectioners' sugar.
- Serve with sour cream and sliced fresh fruit.
- Sauté 2 cups sliced apples in 1 tbs. butter until tender. Stir in 1/4 tsp. cinnamon and spoon over baked oven pancake. Dust with confectioners' sugar.
- Sprinkle top of batter with a mixture of 1 tbs. sugar and 1/4 tsp. cinnamon.
- Add 1 tbs. grated orange rind (zest) and 1/4 tsp. nutmeg to batter.
- Add 2 tsp. grated lemon rind (zest) and 2 tbs. chopped nuts to batter.

CREPES

*Crepes lend themselves well to a variety of presentations and meals. Look for dessert or dinner sauces in **Versatile Syrups, Spreads and Sauces**, page 140-150. Crepes will keep for several days in the refrigerator, wrapped in plastic wrap or foil. Freeze them in stacks, separated by waxed paper, tightly wrapped in foil.*

½ cup milk
½ cup water
2 eggs
1 cup all-purpose flour
½ tsp. salt
vegetable oil (a few drops for each crepe)

Combine all ingredients in a blender container. Blend until smooth. Refrigerate batter for 2 hours or overnight. Heat a crepe pan or small skillet to a fairly high temperature. Brush pan with oil. Pour about 2 tbs. batter into pan. Tilt quickly to coat pan with batter. Pour off excess batter. When browned on the bottom, turn. Cook until brown. Repeat process using the remaining batter. Grease pan between crepes. To serve, fill each crepe with filling and/or top with sauce.

VARIATIONS

- **For dessert crepes**, add the following ingredients to the basic crepe batter.
  1 tbs. brandy
  1/2 tsp. grated orange or lemon rind (zest)
  1 tbs. sugar
- **For fruit crepes**, spoon 1/4 cup sliced fresh fruit or berries on a crepe, fold it twice and dust it with confectioners' sugar.

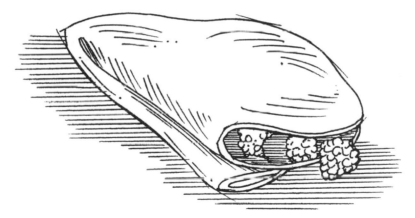

QUICK MIX WAFFLES

Be creative with the numerous waffle variations on page 134.

2 cups *All-Purpose* or *Buttermilk Quick Mix*, page 7
2 tbs. honey or sugar
2 eggs, separated
1 cup milk

Measure *Quick Mix* into a bowl. Mix honey, egg yolks and milk together well. Add liquid mixture to dry ingredients. Stir until just blended. Beat egg whites until stiff and fold into batter. Pour or spoon batter onto a hot waffle iron. Cook waffles to desired doneness.

CRISPY WAFFLES

When you are making waffles, double the recipe and freeze the extras. Pop them into the toaster when you have the urge for a waffle.

1 cup whole wheat or all-purpose flour
1 cup all-purpose flour
1 tbs. baking powder
½ tsp. salt
2 tbs. sugar
2 eggs, separated
6 tbs. butter or margarine, melted, or vegetable oil
1½ cups milk

Stir together flours, baking powder, salt and sugar. Mix egg yolks, butter and milk together well. Add liquid mixture to dry ingredients. Stir until just blended. Beat egg whites until stiff and fold into batter. Pour or spoon batter onto a hot waffle iron. Cook waffles to desired doneness.

WAFFLE VARIATIONS

Add any one of the following ingredients, or changes, to batter.

- ⅔ cup diced banana and ¼ cup unprocessed bran
- ½ cup grated apple and ½ tsp. cinnamon
- ½ cup chopped dates and ¼ cup chopped nuts
- ¾ cup blueberries
- ⅓ cup coconut and ⅓ cup chopped nuts
- ½ cup chopped pecans or walnuts
- ⅓ cup shredded cheddar cheese and ¼ cup crumbled crisp bacon
- replace the milk with buttermilk and add ½ tsp. baking soda
- replace ¾ cup milk with ¾ cup orange juice and add 1 tbs. grated orange rind (zest)

CORN WAFFLES

*Top with **Chili Topper**, page 148, for a great southwestern flavor.*

1½ cups all-purpose flour
½ cup yellow cornmeal
1 tbs. baking powder
½ tsp. salt
2 tbs. sugar
1 cup whole kernel corn (fresh, frozen and thawed or canned)
2 eggs, separated
6 tbs. butter or margarine, melted, or vegetable oil
1½ cups milk

Stir together flour, cornmeal, baking powder, salt and sugar. Mix corn, egg yolks, butter and milk together well. Add liquid mixture to dry ingredients. Stir until just blended. Beat egg whites until stiff and fold into batter. Pour or spoon batter onto a hot waffle iron. Cook waffles to desired doneness.

GINGERBREAD WAFFLES

*Try these waffles topped with warm **Spicy Applesauce**, page 145.*

2 cups all-purpose flour
1 tbs. baking powder
½ tsp. salt
½ tsp. cinnamon
¼ tsp. ground ginger
¼ tsp. nutmeg
2 tbs. sugar
½ cup molasses
2 eggs, separated
6 tbs. butter or margarine, melted, or vegetable oil
1 cup milk

Stir together flour, baking powder, salt, cinnamon, ginger, nutmeg and sugar. Mix molasses, egg yolks, butter and milk together well. Add liquid mixture to dry ingredients. Stir until just blended. Beat egg whites until stiff and fold into batter. Pour or spoon batter onto a hot waffle iron. Cook waffles to desired doneness.

SOUR CREAM WALNUT WAFFLES

These tempting, rich waffles are elegant dusted with confectioners' sugar.

1 cup whole wheat or all-purpose flour
1 cup all-purpose flour
2½ tsp. baking powder
½ tsp. baking soda
½ tsp. salt
⅔ cup chopped walnuts
2 tbs. sugar
2 eggs, separated
6 tbs. butter or margarine, melted, or vegetable oil
1½ cups milk
¾ cups sour cream

Stir together flours, baking powder, baking soda, salt, nuts and sugar. Mix egg yolks, butter, milk and sour cream together well. Add liquid mixture to dry ingredients. Stir until just blended. Beat egg whites until stiff and fold into batter. Pour or spoon batter onto a hot waffle iron. Cook waffles to desired doneness.

DANISH AEBLESKIVERS

Katherine's great grandmother, Christine, brought this recipe and her aebleskiver pan to California from Denmark in the 1890's. The pan was handed down from mother to daughter for generations. Katherine is still using it! An aebleskiver pan has round indentations in which the batter cooks. Serve with butter and jam or syrup.

¾ cup whole wheat or all-purpose flour
¾ cup all-purpose flour
2 tsp. baking powder
½ tsp. salt
1 tbs. sugar
2 eggs, separated

1 cup milk
vegetable oil
aebleskiver pan
sliced bananas or peaches, optional
confectioners' sugar

Stir together flours, baking powder, salt and sugar. Mix egg yolks and milk together well. Add liquid mixture to dry ingredients. Stir until just blended. Beat egg whites until stiff and fold into batter. Heat aebleskiver pan. Spoon ½ tsp. oil into each section and fill ⅔ full with batter. Cook over medium heat until bubbles appear. Turn aebleskivers with a fork or skewer and cook the other side until lightly browned. To vary flavor, add a slice of banana or peach to each before it is turned. Dust with confectioners' sugar.

POPOVERS

Perfect popovers are high and light with a golden brown shell.

1 cup milk
1 tbs. butter or margarine, melted, or
   vegetable oil

2 eggs
1 cup all-purpose flour
1/4 tsp. salt

Preheat oven to 375°. Oil custard cups or muffin cups and preheat in oven. Combine all ingredients and mix until smooth. Fill heated cups 1/2 full with batter. Bake for 45 to 50 minutes. Do not open oven or popovers may collapse. Prick with fork or skewer to let steam escape. Serve immediately.

POPOVER VARIATIONS

- **Whole Wheat** - replace 1/2 cup all-purpose flour with 1/2 cup whole wheat flour
- **Orange Spice** - add 1 tsp. grated orange rind (zest), 1/4 tsp. cinnamon and 1 tsp. sugar
- **Parmesan** - sprinkle top of batter with Parmesan cheese before baking.
- **Cheese** - add 1/4 cup shredded cheese
- **Herb** - add 1/2 tsp. dried basil, thyme, oregano or dill

VERSATILE SYRUPS, SPREADS AND SAUCES

Make your own winning syrups and spreads — you'll find that they are more economical than those commercially prepared, and you'll have more variety. Turn biscuits, waffles or crepes into exciting and out-of-the ordinary dinner treats by serving them with a delicious sauce or topping. The next time you bake a loaf of bread for a gift, include a little pot of one of the sweet or savory spreads.

HOMEMADE "MAPLE" SYRUP

Makes about 1 cup

Make your own syrup and add one of our variations for a special touch.

1 cup brown sugar, firmly packed
2/3 cup water
2 tbs. butter or margarine
1/2 tsp. maple or vanilla extract

Boil brown sugar and water in a saucepan for 5 minutes. Stir in butter or margarine and flavor extract. Serve warm.

VARIATIONS

Add any one of the following ingredients to 1 cup *Homemade "Maple" Syrup*. Heat in a saucepan and serve warm.

- 2 tsp. grated orange rind (zest)
- 1/4 cup chopped pecans and 2 tbs. butter or margarine
- 1/4 cup light cream
- 2 tbs. sherry, 2 tbs. butter or margarine, and dash of cinnamon and nutmeg

HONEY BUTTER SYRUP

Makes about 1 cup

Instead of eating your pancake, waffle or biscuit with cold honey, try this tempting warm syrup.

1 cup honey
¼ cup butter

Heat ingredients in a saucepan over medium heat until butter melts. Serve warm.

VARIATIONS

Add one of the following to *Honey Butter Syrup*.

- ¼ tsp. cinnamon and ¼ tsp. nutmeg
- 2 tsp. grated orange rind (zest)
- ¼ cup shredded coconut and ¼ cup light cream or milk

SWEET AND SAVORY BUTTERS

To make your quick breads extra-special, spread a flavored butter on top.

Add one of the following to ½ cup soft butter. If desired, whip butter with an electric mixer until fluffy.

- ¼ cup honey or maple syrup
- 2 tsp. grated lemon or orange rind (zest) and 1 tbs. powdered sugar or honey
- 1 peach, peeled and chopped, 1 tsp. lemon juice, 2 tbs. brown sugar or honey and a dash cinnamon
- 1 tbs. snipped parsley, ¼ tsp. oregano, ¼ tsp. dill and 1 clove garlic, minced
- 2 tbs. snipped chives or parsley
- 3 tbs. grated Parmesan cheese, ¼ tsp. marjoram and ¼ tsp. basil

HARD SAUCE
Makes about 1 cup

Traditionally served with plum pudding, this sauce is good with many muffins and quick loaves. It can be molded, packed into a ramekin or rolled and sliced.

½ cup butter, softened   ½ tsp. vanilla extract
1½ cups confectioners' sugar   2 tbs. brandy, bourbon or rum

Blend ingredients thoroughly and refrigerate until firm.

SWEET CREAM CHEESE SPREADS

Makes about 1½ cups

Cream cheese spreads are delicious on nut breads.

Add one of the following to 8 oz. softened cream cheese.

- 2 tsp. grated orange rind (zest) and 2 tbs. honey or sugar
- 3 tbs. orange marmalade
- ¼ cup chopped dates or raisins
- ¼ cup chopped nuts
- 3 tbs. maple syrup
- ½ cup mango chutney
- 1 can (10½ oz.) crushed pineapple, drained

TROPICAL FRUIT SPREAD

Makes about 1½ cups

Give your quick breads an island flair with this special spread.

1 tbs. honey or sugar
⅓ cup drained crushed pineapple
1 tsp. grated orange rind (zest)

¼ cup shredded coconut
1 pkg. (8 oz.) cream cheese, softened

Mix ingredients until blended.

FRUIT SAUCE

This sauce is luscious with shortcake, pancakes, crepes or waffles.

2 cups sliced strawberries, bananas or peaches, or cherries or blueberries
1 tsp. grated lemon rind (zest)
2 tbs. butter or margarine
sugar as needed

Heat ingredients in a small saucepan until warm. Taste and add sugar if desired.

SPICY APPLESAUCE

Spoon warm applesauce over crepes, pancakes or waffles.

2 cups applesauce
1 tbs. butter or margarine
½ tsp. cinnamon
¼ tsp. nutmeg

Heat ingredients in a small saucepan until warm.

PESTO SAUCE

Makes about 2 cups

*Pesto adds zip to many foods. Use it in **Pesto Muffins**, page 24, or try it on top of **Pizza Bread**, page 46, with sliced tomatoes or well-drained salsa. It's easy to make, and stores in the refrigerator, tightly covered, for several days.*

2 cups fresh basil leaves
3 cloves garlic
1 cup olive oil
½ cup pine nuts or chopped walnuts
¼ tsp. pepper
½ cup grated Parmesan cheese

With a food processor or blender, process basil, garlic, olive oil, nuts and pepper until a paste forms. Transfer to a bowl and stir in Parmesan cheese.

RATATOUILLE

This bountiful harvest of vegetables is good with herb biscuits or muffins.

1 large white onion, sliced
1 clove garlic, crushed
2 tbs. vegetable oil
1 small eggplant, peeled and cubed
3 medium zucchini, thickly sliced
1/4 lb. fresh mushrooms, halved
3 carrots, peeled and sliced
1 small green bell pepper, cut into strips
2 large tomatoes, skinned and cut into chunks
2 tbs. snipped fresh parsley
1 tsp. salt
1 tsp. dried basil

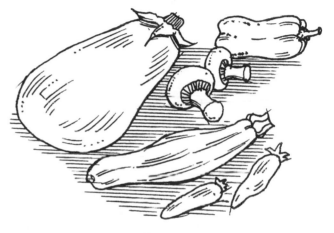

Sauté onion and garlic in oil until tender. Add remaining ingredients and simmer, covered, for about 30 minutes, or until vegetables are cooked. If you like your vegetables tender-crisp, shorten cooking time.

CHILI TOPPER

Makes 4-6 servings

*Serve this topping piping hot over **Corn Muffins**, page 20, **Mexican Cornbread**, page 48, or **Corn Waffles**, page 135.*

1 cup chopped onion
1 clove garlic, crushed
1 tbs. vegetable oil
1 lb. ground beef
1 can (16 oz.) tomatoes with juice
1 can (4 oz.) chopped green chiles
1 tsp. salt

1 tbs. chili powder, or more to taste
1 tsp. ground cumin
1 bay leaf
½ tsp. dried oregano
1 whole small red chile pepper
1 can (16 oz.) red kidney beans, rinsed
    and drained

In a skillet, sauté onion and garlic in oil until tender. Add ground beef and brown. Drain fat. Stir in tomatoes, chiles, salt, chili powder, cumin, bay leaf, oregano and red pepper. Simmer covered for about 2 hours, stirring occasionally. Add a little water if chili is too thick. Add beans and heat until warm. Remove bay leaf and red chile pepper before serving.

SHERRIED CRAB SAUCE

Try this San Francisco favorite over waffles.

2 tbs. butter or margarine
2 tsp. whole wheat or all-purpose flour
1 cup light cream or milk
1 cup crabmeat
salt and pepper to taste
dash nutmeg
3 tbs. dry sherry

Melt butter in a saucepan and stir in flour. Gradually add cream and stir until thickened. Add remaining ingredients and heat until warm.

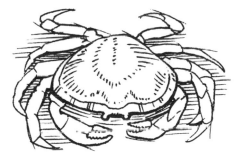

BROCCOLI CHEESE SAUCE

Try this creamy sauce over popovers or biscuits.

1½ cups chopped broccoli
2 tbs. butter
2 tbs. flour
1 cup milk
⅔ cup shredded cheddar cheese
¼ tsp. dry mustard

Steam broccoli or cook, covered, in boiling water for 5 to 7 minutes or until just tender. Drain and set aside. Melt butter and stir in flour to blend. Add milk slowly, stirring until sauce is smooth. Add cheese and dry mustard and continue stirring until cheese is melted. Fold in broccoli and serve warm.

INDEX

SERVE CREATIVE, EASY, NUTRITIOUS MEALS WITH nitty gritty® COOKBOOKS

Entrées From Your Bread Machine
Muffins, Nut Breads and More
Healthy Snacks for Kids
100 Dynamite Desserts
Recipes for Yogurt Cheese
Sautés
Cooking in Porcelain
Appetizers
Recipes for the Loaf Pan
Casseroles
The Best Bagels are made at home*
 (*perfect for your bread machine)
The Toaster Oven Cookbook
Skewer Cooking on the Grill
Creative Mexican Cooking
Extra-Special Crockery Pot Recipes
Cooking in Clay
Marinades
Deep Fried Indulgences
Cooking with Parchment Paper
The Garlic Cookbook
Flatbreads From Around the World
From Your Ice Cream Maker

Favorite Cookie Recipes
Cappuccino/Espresso: The Book of
 Beverages
Indoor Grilling
Slow Cooking
The Best Pizza is made at home*
 (*perfect for your bread machine)
The Well Dressed Potato
Convection Oven Cookery
The Steamer Cookbook
The Pasta Machine Cookbook
The Versatile Rice Cooker
The Dehydrator Cookbook
The Bread Machine Cookbook
The Bread Machine Cookbook II
The Bread Machine Cookbook III
The Bread Machine Cookbook IV:
 Whole Grains and Natural Sugars
The Bread Machine Cookbook V:
 Favorite Recipes from 100 Kitchens
The Bread Machine Cookbook VI:
 *Hand-Shaped Breads from the
 Dough Cycle*

Worldwide Sourdoughs From Your
 Bread Machine
Recipes for the Pressure Cooker
The New Blender Book
The Sandwich Maker Cookbook
Waffles
The Coffee Book
The Juicer Book
The Juicer Book II
Bread Baking (traditional)
No Salt, No Sugar, No Fat Cookbook
Cooking for 1 or 2
Quick and Easy Pasta Recipes
The 9x13 Pan Cookbook
Low Fat American Favorites
Now That's Italian!
Low Salt, Low Sugar, Low Fat Desserts
Healthy Cooking on the Run
The Wok
Favorite Seafood Recipes
New International Fondue Cookbook

For a free catalog, write or call:
Bristol Publishing Enterprises, Inc.
P.O. Box 1737
San Leandro, CA 94577